$\mathcal{L}$osing Your
$\mathcal{P}$ounds
of $\mathcal{P}$ain

Revised Edition

Also by Doreen Virtue, Ph.D.

<u>**Books**</u>

MESSAGES FROM YOUR ANGELS
ANGEL VISIONS II
EATING IN THE LIGHT (with Becky Prelitz, M.F.T., R.D.)
THE CARE AND FEEDING OF INDIGO CHILDREN
HEALING WITH THE FAIRIES
ANGEL VISIONS
*DIVINE PRESCRIPTIONS
HEALING WITH THE ANGELS
*DIVINE GUIDANCE
CHAKRA CLEARING
ANGEL THERAPY
THE LIGHTWORKER'S WAY
"I'D CHANGE MY LIFE IF I HAD MORE TIME"
CONSTANT CRAVING A–Z
CONSTANT CRAVING
THE YO-YO DIET SYNDROME

<u>**Audio Programs**</u>

PAST-LIFE REGRESSION WITH THE ANGELS
*DIVINE PRESCRIPTIONS
THE ROMANCE ANGELS
CONNECTING WITH YOUR ANGELS (2-tape set and 6-tape set)
MANIFESTING WITH THE ANGELS
KARMA RELEASING
HEALING YOUR APPETITE, HEALING YOUR LIFE
HEALING WITH THE ANGELS
*DIVINE GUIDANCE
CHAKRA CLEARING
LOSING YOUR POUNDS OF PAIN (abridged audio book)

<u>**Oracle Cards**</u> (44 divination cards and guidebook)

HEALING WITH THE ANGELS ORACLE CARDS
HEALING WITH THE FAIRIES ORACLE CARDS
MESSAGES FROM YOUR ANGELS ORACLE CARDS

All of the above titles are available through your local bookstore.
All items except those with an asterisk (*) are available by calling
Hay House at: (800) 654-5126.

Please visit the Hay House Website at: **hayhouse.com** and
Dr. Virtue's Website at: **AngelTherapy.com**

Losing Your Pounds of Pain

Breaking the Link Between Abuse, Stress, and Overeating

Doreen Virtue, Ph.D.

Hay House, Inc.
Carlsbad, California • Sydney, Australia
Canada • Hong Kong • United Kingdom

Published and distributed in the United States by:
    Hay House, Inc., P.O. Box 5100, Carlsbad, CA 92018-5100 • (800) 654-5126
(800) 650-5115 (fax) • www.hayhouse.com
    Hay House Australia Pty Ltd, P. O. Box 515, Brighton-Le-Sands NSW 2216
phone: 1800 023 516 • *e-mail:* info@hayhouse.com.au

Editorial supervision: Jill Kramer   •   *Design:* Jenny Richards

Originally published by Hay House, Inc., August 1994.

Library of Congress Cataloging-in-Publication Data

Virtue, Doreen
    Losing your pounds of pain : breaking the link between abuse, stress, and overeating/
Doreen Virtue. -- Rev. ed.
        p. cm.
    Includes bibliographical references and index.
    ISBN 1-56170-950-6 (trade paper)

    1. Compulsive eating. 2. Obesity--Psychological aspects. I. Title.
RC552.C65 V56 2002
616.85'26--dc21   2001052757

ISBN 1-56170-950-6

05 04 03 02   5 4 3 2
1st printing, Revised Edition, January 2002
2nd printing, Revised Edition, May 2002

Printed in the United States of America

Cover art is a modified version of Elly Reeve's oil painting
"You Are Never Alone" (artist e-mail: emreeve@aol.com)

To My Parents, Joan and Bill Hannan,
with love and appreciation

Contents

Preface

Ifirst decided to write this book in 1991 while serving as Program Director of an all-female psychiatric hospital specializing in sexual abuse survivors. Almost every client was struggling with deep emotional pain: stress, grief, depression, rage, and dissatisfaction with work, marriage, and life in general. They expressed, "Is this all my life will ever be?" to me in various ways. These women had turned to food for comfort, security, and sometimes self-punishment. Many were convinced that, if they could only lose the weight, all of their pain would go away. What they came to learn was the opposite: First they had to lose their pain, and then their weight would leave them.

When I initially became a psychotherapist specializing in eating disorders, I was relatively naive about the brutal nature of abusive households. I had never experienced childhood abuse firsthand, but my clients sure had! Woman after woman described various degrees of childhood abuse, including emotional neglect, verbal assaults, molestation, incest, rape, and cult involvement. By the time I'd been a therapist for a year, I'd worked with hundreds of women who cried, screamed, and released pounds and pounds of pain.

Every time I'd work with a woman, she'd lose weight. As a result, my caseload swelled to capacity, filled with women wanting to lose weight. Every one of these women had tried traditional diets, only to regain the weight time and time again.

I was fortunate to grow up in a household surrounded by

loving, extremely intelligent, metaphysically minded parents. My father is a writer, and my mother is a former Christian Science practitioner and Weight Watchers counselor. Is it any wonder that I grew up to be a blend of both their occupations? As a therapist, I've used many of the skills my parents taught me: visualization, affirmations, imagery, meditation, and healthful eating and exercise habits. I used these tools in my 20s to dramatically transform my life from an unhappy existence to one that is something straight out of my dreams today. (But you'll read more about my story later on in this book.)

As a psychotherapist, I worked with clients in the 1980s to discover *why* they were overeating, instead of focusing on *what* they were eating. That was considered a radical approach at the time, but it's readily accepted today. I wrote my second book, *The Yo-Yo Syndrome Diet* (later renamed *The Yo-Yo Diet Syndrome*) based on my research on the link between emotions and overeating.

The methods I used with abuse survivors who compulsively overeat are detailed in the pages that follow. I've geared this book to provide both information *and* real help.

Most of my work has centered around women's issues, and this book reflects that focus. *Losing Your Pounds of Pain* is geared for women struggling with overeating due to stress, depression, anxiety, relationship problems, and career troubles. This book will certainly help men facing these issues as well; pounds of pain, after all, have no gender-based barriers! However, since the majority of people seeking my help are women, this book uses female pronouns such as "she" and "her" instead of awkward phrases such as "he or she" and "him or her."

When I first began speaking and writing about the link between childhood abuse and compulsive overeating, the idea was met with resistance. Today, this concept doesn't seem so far-fetched. However, some therapists seem to have gone overboard in their treatment styles working with eating-disordered clients. It seems that some therapists believe that every eating-disordered client has been sexually abused, even if they have no recollection of the event.

Not every compulsive overeater has been sexually abused! The pain they're carrying, in the form of extra pounds, can stem from a number of sources. Those different sources are described in this book.

On the other hand, there are many abuse survivors who repress and forget about their sexual abuse as a means of coping with the trauma. I am deeply concerned that the current media blitz about "false memories" and overly zealous eating-disorder therapists will negatively impact those people who really need help.

As always, the only approach to healing a problem is an honest examination of its symptoms and roots. Once the pain is identified, it needs to be released. When the pain is released, the pounds will also be. Weight loss will follow.

I strongly believe that our true, natural state is to be light in body and spirit. We are meant to enjoy ourselves and be happy, even while undertaking our responsibilities. Pain is not supposed to be blindly accepted; it is instead a signal that something is wrong and needs to be changed or healed. We are meant to have healthy, normal-weight bodies.

This book will show you how to uncover your true, natural self by shedding the false skin of unhappiness and overweight.

— **Doreen Virtue, Ph.D.,**
Laguna Beach, California

Acknowledgments

I am especially grateful to Louise Hay for her incredible vision and remarkable accomplishments. She has managed to achieve enormous success while helping millions—all the while never letting go of her true self and beliefs. Bravo!

Thank you, too, Reid Tracy, for your enthusiasm, energy, and help in getting this book published. Thank you to Jill Kramer for your editing, and your belief in this project. A special thank you to Dan Olmos, who was there in the beginning . . . and who will always be in our hearts.

PART I

Understanding Your Pounds of Pain

chapter one

BEYOND THE
YO-YO SYNDROME

"The unexamined life is not worth living."
— Socrates

Every extra pound you carry on your body equals a pound of emotional pain you're carrying in your heart. This book will help you shed your excess weight by releasing that pain.

If you've been on many diets and found yourself continually returning to old patterns of unhealthful eating, there may be a psychological cause and cure. I've treated and talked with thousands of women and men who couldn't stop overeating. Always, the overeating was triggered by emotionally painful traumas or situations. Incest. Rape. The death of a parent, grandparent, lover, or spouse. Job problems. Money problems.

Some unpleasant event from the past was acting like a sharp thorn in the paw. These people had lived with the "thorn" for so long that it seemed normal to them. They wanted to accept the pain as "the way it was." But pain is neither normal nor acceptable, and the human response is to seek relief. Many people use food as relief from pain.

In this book, you'll learn the steps my clients used to unblock and release their pain. Once the pain is released, the appetite for food is no longer necessary. The appetite then normalizes, and weight is naturally reduced. This is not an oversimplification. This is based on my clinical experience, as well as well-documented research conducted at respected universities and laboratories around the world.

You'll read about that research in subsequent chapters. The case studies of my clients and workshop attendees illustrate how *you* can benefit from this research.

In my practice, I was involved with near-miraculous recoveries from compulsive overeating, and I'm excited to share the stories of some of these remarkable women and men. They showed enormous courage in their efforts to pull the thorns out of their paws. That action, of course, hurt them tremendously—but just for a short time. After the thorn was removed, the pain lessened.

As you read this book, you may recall events in your own life that you would prefer to forget or not dwell on. I want to state, right here, that I find no value in carrying around pain from the past, or dwelling on abusive childhoods. Many people, sadly, use their history as an abused child as an excuse for unfinished educations and lackluster careers.

There is only one useful purpose for digging up the past: to identify self-blame that is keeping you miserable today. The sad fact is that most children blame themselves when they're abused— "I must be a very bad girl to make Daddy so angry with me." When the abused child grows up, she still carries this self-blame.

The primary purpose of this book, then, is to search-and-destroy any needless self-blame that is holding you back from realizing a bright, light life.

Your True State Is a Normal Body Weight

A happy, content person eats normal amounts of food and stays physically fit. Her body may not be model-thin or athlete-tight, but then she doesn't strive to be "perfect." The happy person has a normal body, and food is simply fuel for daily energy. Food, to a happy person, is not used predominantly for entertainment or comfort.

Anyone who has suffered through an abusive relationship, a life trauma, or excessive stress automatically seeks a way to feel better. Food can provide shelter and a way to block out the awareness of painful memories and uncomfortable emotions. But food is a tool that revictimizes the victim. Being fat carries social consequences that are painful in themselves.

There is nothing wrong with wanting to lose weight and having a healthy body. As I wrote in my book, *The Yo-Yo Diet Syndrome* (Hay House, 1997), when your weight goes up and down, you really see how the world reacts to obesity. When you're thin, you're accorded more respect, admiration, and attention. Men open doors for you and compliment you. When you're overweight, you almost disappear into oblivion. You're no longer special—you're just "average."

The overemphasis on appearance in our society is upsetting, but it's not likely to change anytime soon. Scientific research confirms what we've known all along: Those who are thin are accorded preferential treatment. They're more apt to be hired for a job, and will probably be offered a higher initial salary than an overweight person. They're viewed as being smarter and kinder.

Overweight people are overtly and subtly discriminated against, by both children and adults. The overweight person is in a cycle of pain. The original painful event—whether it was sexual abuse, emotional abandonment by one's parents, an empty marriage, or an unsatisfying career path—pushed the overweight person toward the comfort of food. She gains weight, and then society punishes her for being fat.

I worked as a psychotherapist with people struggling with compulsive overeating for ten years. During that time, I listened to countless stories of pain, which involved everything from unhappy marriages to severe child abuse.

These frustrated overeaters didn't blame their weight on others—far from it. They were simply struggling to find peace of mind. This pain resulted in a mind-set combining discomfort with oneself, sadness, tension, fear, and repressed rage—and was very difficult to live with. Eating brought these people some relief from their anxiety. But after eating, there was simply more anxiety and guilt about gaining weight.

Here's how Rebecca, one of my clients, described this cycle of pain: "I just want to be happy. I don't know *how* to be happy, though. Happiness is almost an abstract concept, you know, something I see in the movies. I've felt it from time to time, like when I was first dating my husband, or when my son was born. To me, happiness means relief from the emptiness and sadness I feel most of the time."

Rebecca remarked that the closest she came to achieving true peace of mind was while eating. "Even then, when I'm eating, I don't feel 100 percent happy. A part of me is watching me pig-out, and I'm just disgusted with myself. I know what overeating does to my weight, but sometimes food is the only thing that makes me feel good."

The good news, though, is that Rebecca and others have replaced overeating with other activities that truly lead to peace of mind and happiness. The process Rebecca went through to lose her pounds of pain is detailed later on in this book.

Dealing with Unresolved Issues

Do you struggle with your weight? Do you sometimes feel hopelessly drawn to eat something even though your mind is screaming, "Don't eat it!"? Do you find that diets and weight-loss programs don't work for you?

If you answered yes to any of these questions, then I'm willing to bet that there's some part of your life that is unresolved. It could be an issue from childhood, or it could be a current situation involving work, finances, or a relationship. Being aware of the situation is a positive first step, but awareness alone won't free you from compulsive overeating.

In my book, *The Yo-Yo Diet Syndrome*, I discussed the link between emotions and overeating, explaining how stress, anger, boredom, and jealousy trigger intense feelings quelled only by food's presence. I also discussed how low self-esteem can lead to compulsive overeating, but I just scratched the surface with that book.

In this book, I delve into the deeper factors leading people to indulge in desperate eating episodes. Here, I discuss how alcoholism in your family background increases the odds you'll overeat foods containing sugar or refined flour. I also cite research studies showing how traumatic sexual experiences can shatter one's self-image. For example, a sexually traumatized girl will hide her healthy, natural state of sexuality, either by covering her body with fat, or by starving her sexuality away.

This book will trigger unconscious processes that will help free you from your pounds of pain. By mentally answering the questions in some of the chapters, you'll undergo some of the work done in psychotherapy, as the material included is almost identical to that which I covered in my therapy sessions.

Feelings will surface as you read case studies about women similar to you. You may feel uncomfortable or saddened by some of the stories, but these are very valuable emotions that needn't be avoided. I promise you that—just as if you were in psychotherapy with me—the discomfort will be supplanted by feelings of relief and peace. So, go through some momentary uneasiness, keep reading the book, and you'll find a rainbow at the end of the path. You're worth the effort.

Different Paths to the Same Place

I'm awestruck by the clear pattern of pain in compulsive overeaters. I didn't start out my career in counseling with the intention of seeking out this pain. Rather, it unfolded in front of me and made itself perfectly obvious.

Every overweight or weight-obsessed person I've worked with has the same "Pounds of Pain" mind-set I discussed earlier. They've all been searching for a sense of relief, peace of mind, and self-acceptance. But, the *way* that they acquired this mind-set differed greatly.

Many had traumatic initial sexual experiences involving date rape, incest, molestation, fondling, or psychological sexual abuse. Other clients had seemingly normal, happy childhoods, with no abuse or alcoholism. However, it turns out that they were emotionally neglected by parents busy with careers or other personal matters.

Those who now find comfort in food often received little solace from relationships. Growing up, they didn't learn how to extract pleasure from interactions with people. Instead, food or material possessions were their primary love objects.

Annette, a 43-year-old manager and divorced mother of two, told me that she'd always felt ugly. She'd never believe men who said, "I love you." Instead, Annette expected that men would leave her for another, more attractive, woman. After all, how could she be pretty with the extra 30 pounds she carried on her small frame?

But the excess weight wasn't responsible for Annette's low self-esteem, as she discovered in therapy: Her feelings of ugliness were keeping her fat. After weeks of therapy and journal writing, Annette understood that her uncle's sexual advances, when she was nine years old, had created a hungry monster inside her.

She recalled, "My uncle would baby-sit for my sister and me, and he would do things to me, things he'd call 'our secrets.' Initially, his advances were on the borderline of being sexual, like giving me a bath or kissing me on the mouth. Then, Uncle Frank began touching my genitals, first on the outside, then he'd put fingers inside my vagina.

"I remember I was real scared. I was afraid of him. He told me my parents would have a bad fight and get divorced if they knew about our special secrets. So I didn't tell anyone.

"Now I understand how much the whole situation disgusted me, and how I turned that feeling into self-disgust. I mean, I blamed myself for the whole thing because I didn't make enough effort to stop Uncle Frank. But what could I have done? I was just a kid, but the incest made me feel like a big, fat nothing!"

Annette's perception of being a "big, fat nothing" influenced every aspect of her life. She didn't expect people to like or respect her, so she made few friends. She felt that her parents and siblings had betrayed her by choosing Uncle Frank as her baby-sitter, leading to strained family relations. And her brief marriage, which yielded two sons, ended after Annette discovered her husband's extramarital affair. Her husband blamed *her:* "You never want sex."

Food was a friend that Annette found she could count on during her painful life—a companion when she was lonely, an entertaining diversion when she was bored. Yet Annette longed to have a satisfying relationship with another person, and she believed that losing weight and looking better was the key to attracting love and friendship. So she'd go on diets once or twice a year. But the moment she'd deprive herself of her best friend, food, Annette's feelings connected to the incest—that is, anger, frustration, and self-hatred—would resurface, masking the real reason that Annette was overweight. It wasn't until she'd gone through therapy that Annette was successfully able to lose, and keep off, her extra 30 pounds.

Once a person becomes trapped in a depression-borne eating cycle, it's difficult to escape without intervention. In the chapters that follow, you'll discover step-by-step methods for decreasing "emotional hunger," which will help eliminate eating binges fueled by depression, grief, guilt, anger, or stress.

The primary purpose of this book, of course, is to lower your emotional hunger. I firmly believe in this statement: The entire issue of overweight stems from problems with the appetite. If you weren't emotionally hungry so much of the time, you wouldn't be eating so much. And if you weren't eating so much, your weight would be normal.

I've identified four primary emotions leading to overeating: Fear, Anger, Tension, and Shame (FATS, or fattening feelings). These feelings are often symptoms of unresolved stress and abuse. While reading this book, you'll learn how to take Fear, Anger, Tension, and Shame and transform them into Forgiveness, Acceptance, and Trust of your Self. And even better—after you release the pain and the accompanying pounds, you'll put the past behind you and Forget All That Stuff!

But first, I'm going to ask you to recall and delve into parts of your past that you may not want to remember. After all, it's not pleasant to examine pain. However, there is a definite purpose to my request. If you're not compulsively overeating, or aren't displaying symptoms of unresolved abuse (depression, insomnia, relationship difficulties, and so on), then I say, "Forget the past right now, and put it behind you!"

But, if you *are* compulsively eating, and traditional dieting methods have frustrated and failed you, then you need to learn from the past before you can put it behind you. Right now, your uncovered pain from the past is triggering your out-of-control eating. I urge you to uncover the pain from the past that robs you of your happiness today, because there is most certainly unresolved anger and distrust created by the abuse in your past. If you're chronically overeating, it's probably the result of anger that you've turned on yourself, and unresolved feelings can leave you feeling depressed, scared, and insecure.

By returning to the original trauma or traumas—even briefly—we'll pull the plug on that unresolved anger. We're going to redirect the anger, outward. Then we're going to work on increasing your trust levels, both in yourself and in others who deserve your trust.

At that point, we're going to release the past, and the pain connected to it. The FATS feelings will then be Forget All That Stuff! And when the pain is released, the fat and excess appetite will no longer be needed. You won't be holding on to anger; you won't be holding on to pain. You won't need to mask these destructive emotions with food and fat, and as a result, your appetite will normalize, and your weight will naturally drop.

The therapeutic work you'll be doing by reading this book will reduce your emotional hunger. You'll lose weight simply because you'll binge and nibble less often. The principles of *Losing Your Pounds of Pain* can be successfully incorporated into any balanced, low-fat, moderate-calorie diet, combined with an exercise program.

Research from such sources as the University of Manchester (U.K.), Cornell Medical Center and the University of Oxford show a clear link between sexual abuse and mood disorders, usually depression. The studies further point to overeating as the chief coping mechanism for depressed sexual abuse survivors. In fact, Cornell reported that obese persons are five times more likely to have mood disorders than normal-weight persons.

Further research from prestigious American and international universities show the phenomenon underscoring the pain/pound link:

- Ten times as many women as men are victims of sexual abuse, the same female-dominated ratio reported in eating disorders (Devine, 1980).

- One study of 54 obese people enrolled in a weight-reduction program found that their rates for mood disorders and current or past psychiatric illnesses—mostly depression and dysthymia—were at least five times greater than those found in the general population (Goldsmith, S. J. 1992).

- Women who experience early (before age 14) sexual intercourse against their wishes are significantly more likely to have eating disorders than women who had first sexual experiences later in life, and/or in accordance with their wishes (Calam, 1989).

- A history of sexual abuse has been reported to be associated with eating disorders two to four times more often than one would expect to see in the general population (Tice, et. al., 1989).

- About 20 percent of American women have eating disorders. I believe the fact that 20 percent of American women are also sexual abuse survivors (Burgess, 1985) is no coincidence.

- Compulsive overeaters report experiencing significantly more life stress than "normal eaters." One study concluded that adolescent overeaters experience 250 times the amount of life stress experienced by adolescents who don't compulsively overeat.

Healing the Unhappiness

As I write this book, there is a dualistic movement in societal awareness about childhood abuse. On the one hand, there's an incredible openness in acknowledging and publicly discussing the topics of incest and rape. However, there is growing suspicion that therapists are planting ideas in the minds of clients, who—because they are supposedly open to suggestion by the therapist—begin to imagine that they were abused as children. In other words, the supposition is that the therapist has falsely created the idea of childhood abuse in the client's mind.

While I have seen damage inflicted by inexperienced and misguided therapists, and I have seen many questionable cases involving child abuse, I don't believe that false abuse memories are widespread. Why would someone conjure up a false memory of childhood abuse? To explain their unhappiness? Someone would have to be truly miserable in order to create these false memories. And if the person *is* that unhappy, chances are that there was some type of childhood abuse.

A child raised with love, safety, and security will naturally grow into a happy adult because happiness is the natural, normal state of being. Although this type of person will occasionally experience mood fluctuations, these are normal and often triggered by outside influences and life stressors. Most of the time however, a well-adjusted person feels content. If someone feels unhappy much of the time, something is definitely wrong.

However, healing the unhappiness doesn't involve blaming others or blaming the past. It *does* involve understanding and learning from the past. It involves acknowledging and understanding the extra pain that led to those extra pounds, and then taking the steps to lose the pounds of pain.

Subsequent chapters describe different hurtful situations most often linked to compulsive overeating, and also suggest ways to break the pain/pound link. These hurtful situations range from the severe to the seemingly ordinary, but the effect is the same: compulsive overeating tendencies.

In every instance, I've tried to make the suggestions practical and easy. I know how many times I've read self-help books filled with complicated advice that I never got around to trying. The suggestions in this book are the same therapeutic assignments I've given clients over the years. Other recommendations were developed at the workshops I've given across the country, advice that has definitely helped workshop attendees lose their pounds of pain.

chapter two

PERFECT CHILDHOODS
AND OTHER MYTHS

"The ultimate lesson all of us have to learn
is unconditional love, which includes
not only others, but ourselves as well."
— Elisabeth Kübler-Ross

Childhood Emotional and Psychological Abuse

Quite often, when I'd be taking a history of a new client, I'd have someone tell me, "I had the perfect childhood. No one hit me, and my parents didn't drink." Now, I'm not a negative person who goes looking for problems where they don't exist, but whenever someone *in therapy*—especially for depression—said that they had a "perfect" childhood, I usually found evidence of childhood emotional abuse. Like other "ghosts" of abuse, emotional abuse is intangible and subtle and is usually only uncovered by tracing adulthood problems back to their original source.

Certainly, all parents make mistakes in raising their children. There is no such thing as "perfect parenting." No parent—in the absence of mental illness or substance abuse—deliberately sets out to harm their child. So, right off the bat I want to distinguish emotional abuse from normal parental mishaps. The chief distinction is that emotional abuse results in lasting scars and negative changes in personality. The adult's *intentions*—good or bad—do not determine whether an action is abusive or not. Again, these definitions are not designed to point fingers at parents, or label someone a "bad person"—that would serve no useful purpose. We are just trying to know ourselves . . . and know our histories.

Let's begin with a common form of emotional abuse: neglect. When reading these examples, stay focused on your own childhood. Don't go into a guilt trip about your own relationship with your children. Now is not the time to look at your own parenting skills (they were learned). By "changing the subject" and worrying about your own parenting habits, you're avoiding looking at your own stuff. That's a very common form of denial and minimization.

For right now, stay focused on yourself. In the long run, that's what will help you. And when you feel better about yourself, you'll naturally be a happier, healthier parent.

Neglected Love

The women you will read about here all suffered from neglect (the most common form of emotional abuse) while growing up. These are not self-pitying, whining women—they're actually proud, self-reliant types. But they're all dealing with the pain of compulsive overeating and relationship problems—resulting from the neglect.

First, there's Melanie:

— When Melanie recalls her childhood, she has an image of her mother vacuuming and cleaning—constantly. "Every minute, she was cleaning the house," remembers Melanie. "She was always in a rush and in a bad mood because she was cleaning after my brothers and me. I remember feeling guilty when she'd wash the dishes right after we ate."

Melanie's mother exhibited perfectionistic and compulsive tendencies toward housework. The woman rationalized that she was being "a good mother and wife" by keeping the house spotless. That was a strong cultural notion then, one that continues today. But there's a difference between maintaining a neat, sanitary home and spending every moment scrubbing and polishing. In the latter situation, the homemaker is usually attempting to keep busy to avoid human contact. Compulsive housekeeping, like workaholism and other addictions, is a way to avoid such intimacy.

Now, since children require emotional connectedness with their parents, those who are raised by "super housewives" are often confused. They seem to have the perfect mother, one who makes great meals and irons their clothes. In the eyes of the world, it may seem that this type of mother is perfect because she keeps an immaculate home and cooks like a French chef. Yet children who grow up in these households are left with an emptiness triggered by the lack of *emotional* mothering (as opposed to *physical* mothering) they receive.

As these kids mature, they try to fill this void with things such as food, which temporarily makes them feel full and numb; and material goods, which are often purchased compulsively. Others may even use people to fill this vacuum, as is the case when some women "collect" boyfriends instead of engaging in one monogamous, intimate relationship.

Here are several case studies of women who came into therapy for weight problems. Every one of these women described feeling empty, incomplete, or unfulfilled with themselves and with their lives. They had turned to eating compulsively in a futile attempt to fill these voids. Of course, feeling full from food temporarily numbs the emptiness inside—but after the food digests a bit, the emptiness returns . . . and with it, an accompanying feeling of self-disgust for going on yet another eating binge.

As you will see from their backgrounds, each woman lacked emotional or psychological nurturing. Their parents were there, physically, but gone emotionally:

— Wanda was neglected by a stay-at-home mother. Wanda's mother was usually passed out on the couch, dead drunk, when the little girl got home from school. Wanda had to entertain herself, since she was too embarrassed to invite friends to the house. One time, she even had to clean up her mother's vomit after a drinking binge. Wanda's mother was physically there, every day, but she was never emotionally there for her daughter.

— Edwina's mother, like Wanda's, was chemically dependent. But Edwina's mother denied she had any problem because the drugs she used were prescribed by her doctor. Nonetheless, the tranquilizers made her moods unstable, and she'd often scream at Edwina and her sister for inconsequential reasons. Most of the time, though, Edwina's mother stared blankly in front of her in a drug-induced stupor.

Joyce's pain is known far too well by far too many women. Although not technically abuse, I'm putting her case in this section because it's so widespread.

— Joyce never felt she got enough from her father. As a result, she sought out men who reminded her of her dad: aloof, distant, and unemotional. Unconsciously, she was seeking her dad's love and approval through these men. She tried to change these standoffish men into warm lovers, believing that if she tried hard enough, the men would alter their behavior. Not surprisingly, Joyce ended up leaving these men because her emotional needs went unmet.

I'm not blaming fathers for this common scenario, or saying that they're "bad" or they played out this type of behavior on purpose. But many women feel empty or wounded because their fathers didn't express enough love, affection, and approval to their daughters.

— In Mary Ann's case, her father suffered from manic depression, a mental illness that can wreak havoc on family members. One minute, her father would be an energetic, charismatic "buddy-type" dad, and the next, he'd isolate himself, hiding behind his closed bedroom door. Mary Ann never knew what to expect from her father's mood swings, so she constantly walked on eggshells just in case Dad was in one of his moods. To this day, she has difficulty relaxing around male authority figures.

— Angela was the oldest of five children. Since her mother was bedridden with a debilitating chronic illness, Angela functioned as the family caretaker. She neglected her schoolwork to shop and cook the family's dinners, and she made sure her mother was cared for. Angela also looked after her younger siblings, coaching them to do their homework, while her own remained unfinished.

Angela's adulthood followed the same course: She took care of everyone but herself. "Taking care of others is the right thing to do," was her deepest belief, along with fears of "being selfish" if she did anything nice for herself. While being kind, thoughtful, and loving are virtuous credos that many of us try to uphold, Angela's situation was quite different.

Deep down, Angela resented others. She resented them for "taking advantage" of her niceness, and also because no one took care of her needs. She used food as her weapon to fight back, along with the frequent arguments she had with her husband.

When Angela's weight topped 200 pounds, she finally sought help. In therapy, Angela learned how to balance the longing to take care of her family with her need to get her own desires met. She learned how to enjoy simple pleasures such as taking the kids to the park or baking bread with her daughter. Instead of resenting her caretaking activities, she began to appreciate them.

Angela redefined the word *selfishness* and began taking time for herself. The result was that both Angela and her family benefited from her new outlook on life. She became a happier, more satisfied wife and mother—definitely more easygoing and fun to be around.

She lost weight through her exercise program, and as her appetite lessened, her resentment and frustration level diminished.

— Like Angela, Rosie felt that she'd missed out on her childhood. An only child, Rosie was raised by a single mother who decided that her daughter would be her best friend and mentor. Rosie's mother shared intimate details about her relationships with men, and consistently asked her daughter for advice on matters of the heart.

Unfortunately, Rosie was emotionally unprepared to function as her mother's peer. She needed to be mothered, not *be* a mother. What Rosie's mother did is called "parentifying" her child. In other words, she was pressuring her child to take on the role of the parent. Parents who are emotionally immature, chemically dependent, or who have personality disorders such as narcissism commonly parentify their children.

For Rosie, insufficient parenting led to anger and feelings of sadness. She felt as if she'd been "ripped off" from having a real childhood. She despaired the lack of a normal mother-daughter relationship, and as an adult, she resented it when her mother asked for small favors, such as a ride to the doctor or store. Rosie would feel furious inside and think, *I don't want to take care of her! After all, she didn't take care of me all those years!*

Instead of confronting her mother with her feelings, though, Rosie kept them to herself. She ate to feel better, primarily bingeing on "comfort foods" such as breads, cookies, mashed potatoes, and cheeses. The texture of these foods, combined with the mood-elevating properties that are common to carbohydrates (more about this in later chapters), pacified temporarily. But in the long run, Rosie's harbored anger and grief resulted in her overeating 45 extra pounds onto her body.

In contrast, Jean's situation doesn't involve abuse or neglect in the strict sense of the word. But I've included her story, as well as the story about Charlene that follows Jean's, in this chapter because it illustrates other ways in which parents inadvertently prompt their children's overeating.

— Jean's mother was the picture of a sweet, loving woman. She doted on her children, spending hours playing and talking with them. Jean learned a lot from her mother, including the pleasures and rewards derived from eating. You see, Jean's mother equated food with love—a connection she learned from her own mother, and which she then passed along to Jean.

Whenever Jean would do anything well, such as bringing home an A on a report card or cleaning up her room, she would be rewarded with food. There were M&M's for completing her homework on time, cupcakes for vacuuming the living room, and potato chips for walking the dog.

As an adult, Jean wasn't able to break the food-as-reward connection until she got into therapy. Prior to therapy, every time she'd try to diet, she'd feel deprived. This made sense to her once she understood the significance she'd placed on food: To Jean, since food was a reward, then diets represented a form of punishment.

— Charlene also learned to overeat as a child. The youngest of 11 children, Charlene was part of a big family struggling to make ends meet. At dinnertime, there never seemed to be enough food. The moment that dinner was put on the table, Charlene's older brothers would fight to see who could eat as much as possible. As a result, Charlene learned to scramble to get her share of the meal.

In adulthood, Charlene entered into therapy with me in an effort to understand her compulsive overeating habits. Once she came to terms with her deep-seated fears that "there won't be enough food for me to eat," she was able to curtail her eating. After all, as a parent with a small, financially secure family, Charlene was now able to eat as much food as she wanted. (Unfortunately, she'd done just that and had gained 75 pounds after she got married.) However, as she worked on releasing the fear that she'd go hungry unless she stuffed herself with food, Charlene gradually lost her excess weight.

— Michelle was also taught unhealthy early childhood lessons about food's purpose, but in a different way from Jean or Charlene.

Both of Michelle's parents were highly ambitious entrepreneurs. Her father was in charge of sales and marketing for an international pharmaceutical manufacturer—a job that required extensive travel—and her mother was a successful real estate broker who worked seven days a week. During her rare moments at home, Michelle's mother was usually on the telephone setting appointments and closing deals.

Michelle was an only child— "I always wondered why my parents bothered to have a child, since they were never around"—who was raised by a housekeeper. "My memories of my parents are of seeing them between business trips and appointments," Michelle recalled.

Perhaps to assuage their guilt, Michelle's parents showered her with expensive gifts and clothing, so all her material needs were met. Unfortunately, Michelle went hungry—emotionally hungry. She was unwittingly taught to fulfill her normal human needs for love and affection using material objects. If she was lonely, she'd turn to her dolls, makeup table, or the refrigerator in order to feel better.

As an adult, Michelle continued this external focus. She had difficulties with men—as soon as the relationship started to get serious, she'd break it off. Her fear of intimacy was intertwined with an intense desire for love and security. But since she'd never learned how to interact with people, Michelle's closest friendship was with the food she binged on. Her weight fluctuated by 30-pound swings throughout her adult life until she entered therapy and worked on her fear of intimacy.

— Patty was a remarkable woman who reminded me of the song "Tears of a Clown." She was one of those bubbly, effervescent people who was constantly smiling and doing things to please others. I believe that she genuinely enjoyed making others smile and laugh. At work, she was everyone's favorite co-worker—taking time to listen, bringing in homemade cookies, remembering everyone's birthday.

The only problem was that Patty wasn't taking time to make herself happy, and that's why she entered therapy.

Her childhood was a remarkable story of survival. As the oldest of two sisters raised by a promiscuous, alcoholic mother who would regularly leave her children alone to fend for themselves, Patty remembered many instances where, as a young child, she'd have to figure out how to feed herself and her sister. If there was no food in the house, the hungry little girl would have to beg neighbors for meals.

Sometimes Patty's mother would pile the little girls in the car and take them to bars. Patty and her sister would wait in the locked car for hours while her mother hung out in the bar getting drunk and looking for boyfriends.

They lived in a run-down, unkempt house, so Patty was too embarrassed to invite friends over. She also felt "less than" the other children at school. Her whole childhood was marked by neglect and abandonment. Even more disheartening was how Patty dealt with her trauma: She blamed herself. Instead of being angered by her mother's alcoholic behavior, Patty felt that her mother was justified in mistreating her. "If I had been a better little girl, my mom would have been home more," was the way Patty recalled her childhood. Sadly, children often take responsibility in this way for their parents' behavior.

Unfortunately, Patty grew up feeling responsible for everyone else's welfare. She reluctantly complained to me that she felt overworked at her job, and that she was working more overtime than she cared to. When we examined the root cause of her overburdened feelings, I wasn't too surprised to discover that Patty had volunteered to complete a female co-worker's paperwork each afternoon. This selfless act allowed the co-worker to leave the office early to meet her boyfriend for dates, but since Patty wanted this co-worker to like her, she took on more work than she was capable of handling.

Patty's martyrdom led to time inequities for herself and her family. She'd get off work at 6:00 or 6:30, rush to the grocery store, and try to have dinner ready by 7:30. With no free time, Patty never exercised, and she overate as a way of unwinding from the day's stress. No wonder Patty was unhappy with the 75 extra pounds on her 5'2" frame.

Reframing Neglect and Abuse

Therapy for Patty consisted of "unlearning" the lessons of childhood. As an adult, she tried to objectively step back and view her mother's behavior as stemming from the disease of alcoholism. Once Patty *understood*—not just intellectually, but emotionally—that even if she had been a perfect child, her mother still would have behaved in the same fashion, Patty quit blaming herself.

What follows is a therapy session that I conducted with Patty, in which we started to work through her buried feelings connected to her mother's abandonment:

Therapist (me): Patty, I'd like to ask you to think about your own daughter, April, for a minute. She's ten years old, which is about the age you were when your mother began leaving you alone, right?

Patty: Yes, that's right.

Therapist: Can you describe what it would be like if you left April alone and went on a two-week vacation with your husband?

Patty: You mean without a baby-sitter?

Therapist: That's right, April would be left completely alone in the house for two weeks.

Patty: But—I mean—I would never—

Therapist: And, what's more, during that two weeks, you won't leave much food in the house, and you won't leave any money for her.

Patty: But—

Therapist: You also won't tell any of the neighbors to look after her, and you won't call to check up on her.

Patty: Why would I do something like that?!

Therapist: In addition, you won't tell April where you're going, or how she can get a hold of you during an emergency.

Patty: That's absolutely crazy! Nuts! I can't understand why you would even ask me to think about something like this!

Therapist: Please tell me how that imaginary scenario is any different from what you went through when you were April's age.

Patty: Well, it *is* different. That was very different.

Therapist: How was it different?

Patty: Well, I was a lot stronger than April is.

Therapist: Really?

It took quite a bit of discussion before Patty's years of denial, and defense of her mother's behavior caught up with her. And when it did hit, it hit hard.

Patty (crying): I can't believe that my mother would actually do something like that to us!

In the process of working with clients who have endured years of childhood abuse and abandonment, I've witnessed this sequence of events countless times. There is real griefwork involved in mourning the loss of a happy, safe childhood. Here are the steps involved with that griefwork:

1. Remember the events. It's helpful to write them down in narrative form, as if you're telling someone a story.

2. Step back from the situation and view it objectively. The easiest way to do this is to put another child— your own son or daughter, for example—in your place. Imagine that child enduring the things you went through.

3. Ask yourself: How much is this child responsible for the abuse or abandonment? How much is the adult responsible for the abuse or abandonment?

4. Once the answer comes to you, pay attention to your feelings. You may experience feelings of intense anger directed toward the adult. Don't shut the anger down, no matter how scary it feels to you. This anger, held inside of you all these years, is the primary source of your overeating, as well as any depression nagging at you.

5. Let the anger out. Talk about it with a trained professional—someone who will just listen and not offer any advice or try to "console you." Put your angry thoughts down on paper. Get it out of you. But stay focused on the source of your anger—don't allow yourself to turn the anger back on yourself. Many clients I've worked with "shut down" their anger by focusing on their own children and thinking, *Gee, have I been a bad parent myself?* Right now, focus on your own childhood. In the long run, releasing this anger will make you a better, happier parent.

   The main fear with respect to anger is that you will "lose control" and act out of rage. Many clients have expressed a fear that their anger will make them tear down a building or beat someone up. Don't worry—pent-up anger is much more dangerous than released anger. You won't lose control.

6. As I've stated before, blaming your parent won't solve anything, and it may even make things worse. Even though your parent or other adult perpetrator acted irresponsibly toward you, it's important to view them as a "sick," not a "bad" person. You'll feel

more settled if you reframe your childhood in these terms. Otherwise, you'll resent your parent for the rest of your life, and the resentment will eat you alive. Better to pity that person than to hate them.

The bottom line is this: Unleash yourself from feeling responsible for your childhood pain. You were a child, innocent and naive. The pain was inflicted on you by a sick (mentally ill, depressed, or chemically dependent) adult. *You* did not cause the abuse or neglect. You certainly did not deserve it. And, now that you're an adult, you don't need to carry the burden of childhood pain any longer.

You can release the pain. It's okay to feel good about yourself.

Healing the "Raggedy Ann Syndrome"

Many people who were abused in childhood feel that they carry the equivalent of a "Scarlet Letter" around their necks.

— Patty (from the account above) remembered being called "white trash" by her childhood friend's mother, and she carried that label with her into adulthood. Even though she and her husband lived in a respectable neighborhood with a very comfortable income, Patty couldn't shake her feeling of being "less than."

"It's like others can see right through me," Patty told me. "Even though I drive a nice car and wear nice clothes, I still feel like that raggedy little girl wearing outfits bought at the Salvation Army."

Do *you* ever feel that way? As if you're somehow "damaged" or "not as good as others"? This phenomenon is what I call the "Raggedy Ann Syndrome." It means that you're hanging on to an outdated image of yourself. You are owning, and taking responsibility for, a false picture of who you are as a person.

You are not damaged. You are a complete and perfect person. You are lovable, and deserving of the respect of others. It's so important not to waste the precious time remaining in your life by hanging on to pain that happened in the past. I'm not asking you to forget the past or pretend it didn't happen. (Unfortunately, repressing a memory only adds to the pain; it doesn't lessen it.)

Instead, I'm asking you to understand your past. First, understand it intellectually by allowing the memories to surface. Next, understand it emotionally by seeing that you—as a little girl—were not responsible for the actions of those adults or older children who hurt you. See the situation in the bright, clear light of reality.

Then, wipe your slate clean and start over. Know that there's nothing wrong with you. Go even further, and see how the pain you endured has actually made you an empathetic, caring, and understanding individual.

Perhaps, like many abuse survivors, you've turned your painful lessons into a benefit for society. The majority of the abuse survivors I've worked with have become helping professionals: nurses, therapists, teachers, and social workers. However, part of the reasoning behind their career choice is based on unhealthy needs, and part on healthy ones.

If you want to help others as a way of avoiding your own pain, that's unhealthy. If you enjoy helping others because you feel you're responsible for making others happy or whole, that's not healthy either. But if you want to help others as a way of making sense out of your own pain—wonderful! This is a root principle in the branch of philosophy called "existentialism." Existentialists believe that pain is an inevitable part of being human. A lot of the pain, these philosophers say, has to do with the knowledge that we will inevitably die and then be "nothing."

They say the best way to deal with this pain is to first acknowledge its existence. In other words, admit to yourself that you fear that your life will be meaningless. Then, say the existentialists, you must do something about it. You must *create* meaning in your life.

For myself, my clients, and many of my friends, the way we've created meaning in our lives is through practical application of the lessons that pain has taught us. For example, I suffered through two painful child custody battles many years ago. The pain was tremendous, especially when at one point my ex-husband took our two sons and left the state with no forwarding address. For a time, I had no idea where my children were. I also suffered when others blamed me for the divorce and subsequent custody battle.

I could have dealt with my emotional pain by turning it on myself and becoming depressed. Actually, for a short time, I *did* start to compulsively overeat, and I gained 30 pounds during the custody battle. Fortunately, I recognized what I was doing and turned the situation around.

I went to the bookstore and looked for a self-help manual that would ease my pain while I fought to be reunited with my children, but there were no books on the topic. I was unpublished at the time, and only held a two-year associate's degree in psychology. But I promised myself, "If I get through this custody situation, I'm going to write a book to help others survive the pain."

The pain was, indeed, intense, but eventually my ex-husband and I settled our differences and today, many years later, we have an amicable joint custody arrangement. I went on to interview hundreds of other mothers and fathers in various stages of custody battles, and compiled the stories of emotional pain they shared with me (along with my own story), into a book called *My Kids Don't Live with Me Anymore: Coping with the Custody Crisis* (CompCare Publishers, 1988; now out-of-print).

I think you get my point: You can see your pain as an enemy or as a teacher. I was involuntarily schooled in "what it's like to go through a child custody battle" because I went through it myself. Now, I could have hidden this painful lesson from others—believe me, the societal scorn I experienced during the custody battle made me feel embarrassed to even admit I was involved in such an ordeal. However, I felt that my circumstances had made me uniquely qualified to write a book to help others through the nightmare I had just survived.

The interesting thing about this whole situation is that even though the child custody battle was the most painful thing I've ever endured, writing *My Kids Don't Live with Me Anymore* gave me one of the greatest highs of my life. The writing process—both for my kids, who helped me with one of the chapters—and myself, was extremely cathartic and healing. The publicity tour for the book afforded me the opportunity to meet other parents across the country. And the letters I've received from mothers and fathers who were helped by the information in that book have touched me immensely.

Pulling Yourself Up

When I first decided to write about my child custody experiences, I wasn't sure I could do it. I didn't really believe in myself that much, but I forced myself to try. The first four publishers I sent the book to rejected it right away. I then told myself, "Oh, well, you weren't meant to be a writer" and put the manuscript away in a drawer.

It was only months later, when Pepperdine University invited me to speak about the custody issue at an international conference of therapists, that I thought, *I guess there is some interest in this topic.* I pulled out the manuscript again, and this time, I sent off copies to 30 different publishers.

I got 25 rejections, but I also got five acceptances! I had forced myself to act on my desire to be published, even when I really didn't believe in myself 100 percent. And it worked!

So, have confidence that *you* can achieve your goal of ridding yourself of your pounds of pain! Don't limit yourself in any way.

As you know, pulling yourself up and making yourself "go for it" is like swimming against the tide. Not only do you have your own Raggedy Ann Syndrome to contend with, but, as an overweight person, you must also buck societal intolerance. (We'll discuss fat prejudice in more detail later on.) For now, I just want to assure you that I realize how difficult it is to feel good about yourself when you've got negative forces penetrating your self-esteem.

You've got to start somewhere, though. Giving up and saying, "What's the use? I'll always be fat and miserable," only guarantees one thing: You'll stay overweight *and* unhappy. Of course, it is possible to be overweight *and* happy. But, in most cases, if you're truly happy, you will naturally lose excess weight because you won't be emotionally hungry so much of the time!

So, let's slowly begin to turn the tide in favor of *you*. You're working through your pounds of pain by acknowledging childhood trauma, then releasing feelings of guilt and self-blame. Then, you're releasing pent-up anger and turning the anger away from yourself and toward the appropriate source. You're acknowledging the adults who were responsible for mistreating you, but instead of blaming them, you're seeing them as sick individuals in need of help. The important thing to remember is: Don't be angry at yourself, and don't sustain resentment against you.

Release the negative feelings. There's never going to be a perfect time to get on with your life and feel better about yourself. Although it's a struggle and not fun to think about, you're actually investing in your future by working on these issues right now.

Keep going.

chapter three

BREAKING OUT OF
SELF-MADE PRISONS

"To thine own self be true."
— William Shakespeare

Married to Pain

I often worked with clients who were looking for the source of their pain, and I'd see near-miraculous healings occur. When the victim quit blaming herself and instead turned her anger toward the perpetrator or the situation—and then released that anger—it was like removing a nail from a tire. The excess weight deflated right before my eyes.

Let me tell you about Cindy as an example.

Cindy's Story

The 43-year-old brunette schoolteacher came to me to lose the 100 extra pounds she carried on her 5'4" frame. Cindy was a sweet-voiced woman, intelligent and poised. As she spoke with tight lips and a clenched jaw, I sensed tremendous anger in her voice, mannerisms, and vocabulary. There was a sarcastic edge to her stories, which contrasted oddly with the schoolmarm sweetness she'd carefully cultivated. This was clearly a very tense woman who overate to try to calm her frazzled nerves.

Cindy's husband of 18 years, Ralph, was a traveling salesman who would only come home on weekends. Cindy and Ralph slept in separate beds and had stopped having sex ten years before, when Ralph admitted to a one-night stand while on a sales call. Not surprisingly, both Cindy and Ralph began putting on weight after the extramarital affair. They were sublimating anger, resentment, bitterness, and unmet sexual needs through overeating. Both were avoiding dealing with the issues central to their marriage.

Cindy had been contemplating divorce since Ralph confessed to his adultery, but she kept postponing making a final decision. For ten years, Cindy had been seesawing over the "should I or shouldn't I?" questions concerning divorce. On the one hand, Ralph brought in a great income, and his absence during the week allowed Cindy plenty of time for leisure activities and relaxation. And, she rationalized, with this extra weight on her body, she probably couldn't find a replacement husband very easily. But on the other hand, her marriage was now an empty sham, a marriage of convenience—without even the joy of sex to hold it together. She and Ralph were more like roommates than marriage partners.

As I've said before, I see divorce as a last-ditch solution to marital problems. It is best for a couple to undergo counseling before deciding to separate, especially if children are involved. Fortunately, Cindy and Ralph had never had children. I urged Cindy to bring in Ralph for marital counseling sessions, and I even agreed to arrange for a second therapist to provide marriage counseling if she wanted to keep me as her own private therapist. But Ralph refused to come in, even for a weekend session.

Gradually, I watched the inevitable occur: Cindy asked Ralph to leave home for good. I supported Cindy through her difficult decision and helped her go through the grieving process. What was remarkable was that as soon as she decided unequivocally that she was "absolutely positively" divorcing her husband, Cindy's weight started dropping off like a swiftly deflating beach ball.

Her figure changed from unshapely and round to svelte and attractive because she had taken the nail out of her tire, removed the thorn from her paw.

It's important to note, though, that this wasn't a simple cause-and-effect situation such as, "Get a divorce, lose 100 pounds." Cindy experienced the normal grieving process associated with the loss of her "roommate," and she worked hard in therapy to honestly confront her wide range of feelings. What made the situation a little more palatable was that Cindy had been emotionally prepared for the divorce, which helped to alleviate her grief considerably. Also, the fact that Ralph was agreeable to the divorce (he was also ready) made the transition easier to endure.

In essence, Cindy lost weight by becoming honest with herself. She overcame her fears of losing Ralph and admitted that they both had to shed their deadened sham of a marriage.

We all have, deep inside of us, a picture of what our life is supposed to be like. If our actual existence differs sharply from that dream life, we experience internal conflict—that is, we make ourselves sick or eat or drink too much when we avoid *admitting to ourselves that our life is very different from our fantasies.*

For Better or Worse?

I remember when my own life was a nightmare, far removed from what I had envisioned it to be. You may remember my earlier mention of the warm, loving household I grew up in, and then my first experience with abuse—of the emotional, verbal, and psychological variety—when I was in my early 20s. I was a relatively uneducated housewife, married to a man who screamed at me. He berated me for everything from my not having the coffee ready on time, to my taking too long to go grocery shopping. Nothing I did was right, and my self-esteem hit rock-bottom.

No wonder I was overweight! I overate in order to suppress the voices deep inside me, the ones screaming, "This isn't what your life is supposed to be like! Get out now!" I found that if I didn't eat continually, I would become all too conscious of the deep emptiness, the incredible sadness, surrounding my life and marriage.

Now there's nothing shameful about being a housewife, and nothing wrong with only having a high school diploma. It's just that *I* wasn't happy in this circumstance. Deep inside, I could see how my life was supposed to be as clearly as if I were watching it on television: I was supposed to have a peaceful, calm marriage like my parents, and where my career was concerned, I knew that my true purpose was to write self-help books that blended my metaphysical upbringing in Christian Science and Religious Science with a new understanding of medicine and psychology. I also "knew" that I was supposed to write while living near the water, and that my body was supposed to reflect happiness and health at a normal weight.

I had a lot to change!

At the time, I had very little belief in myself. My husband's incessant put-downs coupled with the added burden of never having enough money ate away at my self-esteem. Even though I had achieved top grades in school and had skipped the fifth grade, I felt very stupid. I kept thinking, *If I were really smart, I wouldn't be so broke and unhappy!* And we were very, very impoverished: barely able to make the rent, and paying the utility bills every month just in the nick of time before the electricity and phones were due to be shut off. At times, we lived on potatoes and macaroni because we couldn't afford anything else.

I felt ugly, stupid, and incompetent. My husband had done a great job of convincing me that no other man would want me, so I might as well stick with him. He was slowly poisoning my whole life, and I had to escape somehow!

Life Is But a Dream

I wanted to be a psychologist and a writer, but how could I dare to believe that I could achieve such lofty goals? It almost seemed as if authors were born genetically different from people like me, as if they had some extra chromosome enabling them to get published. Yet, that fire inside me wouldn't quit burning—pushing me, urging me, to change my life to coincide with my dreams. I realized that I had two choices: stay in my current situation and get fatter and more miserable, or start working toward that vision of authoring books by the water.

Maintaining the mental picture of where I was going was an important first step for me. Each of us has a mission or purpose, and deep inside, we know what that purpose is. I believe that God has plans for us before we're born, and He makes sure we're equipped with the tools to fulfill His mission. We can "see" His mission if we listen very closely.

Of course, everyone's life purpose doesn't involve fame or fortune. I had one client who said his goal in life was to be the world's best tire changer. He meant it!

If you even have a glimpse of what your purpose is supposed to be, it's like a thread you can yank on that will lead you closer to your "big picture." Pull on this thread through solitary meditation, perhaps while walking, exercising, or showering. Concentrate on the mental picture of your dream life until you can see all the details. Don't force the picture to come into focus. Allow it to rise to the surface until it "clicks," and you know this is truly something coming from deep inside of you.

The next thing that commonly occurs after a vision of the dream life appears is that negative thinking rears its ugly head. I kept thinking, *I'm not special enough to ever get published,* and *College will take too long,* and *How can I ever afford to live near the water?*

All these negative thoughts were lies that I had accepted as truth. I had to remember that God wouldn't have given me my dream if He hadn't also given me the tools to fulfill it. I had to believe in His strength, because I didn't seem to have much of my own at that time.

So, I used affirmations to boost my self-esteem. I couldn't afford to buy an affirmation tape at the store, so I made my own.

Looking back, I see that that was the best thing I could have done, as research points to the power that our own voice has on our unconscious. I was also able to tailor the affirmations to fit my personal dream and goals.

I affirmed hundreds of positive thoughts on that cassette tape, and I put down every dream I could think of, from my desire to have a great figure, to my intention of living near the water. I learned that the best way to state affirmations is to declare your dreams and desires as if they're already true. It's the "act as if" principle. Instead of saying, "I would like to have a great figure," you say, "I *have* a great figure."

Another important point is that affirmations are always voiced in positive terms. For example, you'd say, "I enjoy eating healthful foods," as opposed to the negatively worded phrase, "I avoid eating junk food." They both say basically the same thing, but the former affirmation programs your unconscious much more powerfully than the latter.

In Chapter 11, you'll find affirmations that you can incorporate into your own tape.

Anyway, I made myself listen to that tape two or three times a day. At first, all my negative thoughts came rushing forward. I'd listen to an affirmation such "I am a bestselling author," and my unconscious would say, "Oh, this is so stupid; it will never work." My negative thinking was like an out-of-shape muscle groaning in response to a new exercise program. But I kept going.

Gradually, I found myself spontaneously "hearing" my affirmations during the day. I'd be doing housework, and I'd think, *I deserve good*—a thought that came straight from my tape! By the fourth week of listening to my affirmations, I was clearly seeing that it was possible to transform my life. Yes, I was still a little scared, intimated, and unsure—a product of the emotional abuse my husband had inflicted upon me—but I forced myself to persevere, knowing that I had no other choice. At times, I almost felt as if I were being led down a dark hallway and I simply had to trust that I'd be safe when I reached my destination.

The result of my efforts was that my weight began to drop dramatically as I let go of nervous nibbling and stress snacking. However, as my figure started to improve, my husband became jealous and suspicious. He was sure that I was losing weight to attract another man, but I didn't allow his insecurities to cloud my own vision.

I enrolled in college and soon received my first *A*. I was shocked, because I'd forgotten that I was smart! I had replaced the true picture of myself as smart and competent with my husband's lie (designed to keep me from leaving him) that I was worthless and that no other man would ever want me. He had eroded my self-confidence so subtly that I hadn't even noticed that he had been tiptoeing around in my brain like a burglar, robbing me of my self-confidence! Now I was reclaiming what was rightfully mine: my self-worth—and my life. I was granted a $2,500 student loan and used that money to move away from my husband.

Fast-forward to the present day: I now hold four college degrees in psychology; am a bestselling author; have been on many national talk shows; have a healthy, attractive body; a wonderful marriage; and live and write near the water. My current life is almost identical to the picture I had in my head. Magic? No. I certainly had to work hard. But because I was on the right track, I was able to realize my highest goals. You can do the same.

Getting on the Right Track

I've found that when we're on the "right track," the world lets us know. Things go smoothly and easily, even if we're working long and hard hours. Doors seem to open. However, when we're on the wrong track—not fulfilling our mission or purpose—the world also gives us plenty of feedback. It's amazing how many things go wrong when the overall picture of our life is off base.

Our appetite for food is usually an accurate reflection of whether we're on the right track or not. When we're living a false life, one that runs counter to our deep, inner vision, we crave food. Instead of healing our life, we mask our problems with the bandage known as food. We act like prisoners who, in order to better deal with a miserable state of existence, turn to drugs to numb the reality of life.

Did you know that you have the right to change your life for the better? Did you know that no one else but you is going to give you "permission" to change your life? Did you also know that you can start making those changes *right now?*

I ask these questions because when I was living the lie of trying to be an overweight, unhappy, uneducated housewife, I didn't think I had the right to make any changes. I felt like a prisoner stripped of personal freedom. I was waiting for some "authority figure" to say, "Okay, Doreen, now it's time to take the steps toward having a happy life." But that was never going to happen, because God and I were the only ones who knew what my inner dreams were.

The authority figure, the permission-giver, was deep inside of *me!* I discovered the good news: I had the right to decide how to live my life. I had the right to change my life to fit my inner mission. And so I did—thank God!

Reclaiming the Joy of Marriage

By no means am I advocating divorce, separation, or breaking up as a means to a happy life or weight loss. I've worked with many women who falsely blamed their husbands for being the source of their unhappiness.

— One client of mine, Belinda, was convinced her life would be perfect if she got a divorce. She did, and she was even more miserable! After the divorce, Belinda still had all of her old issues because she was the source and originator of the problems—not her husband. On top of that, her divorce created new challenges: financial hardships, moving to a smaller apartment, loneliness, and child-custody problems.

Divorce isn't a miracle cure for problems or overeating. But when a marriage *is* unhappy, something has to change. The first step, when symptoms of a sick relationship occur, is to seek professional help. Some of the indicators include frequent arguments, tense silences, lack of sexual desire, picking on one another, and, of course, physical expressions of anger.

Sometimes people use their marriage as an excuse for everything negative that they feel about their lives: "If only it weren't for my bad marriage, then I'd be happy," or "If only it weren't for my husband, I'd have that great job." Instead of taking that giant (and often intimidating) leap toward changing their lives for the better, these folks spin their wheels in the mud of blame. It's a way of remaining at an endless impasse. Since your spouse is to blame, you don't have to take any responsibility for your own unhappiness.

But guess what? (You probably already know what I'm going to say.) Your spouse is not responsible for whether or not you're pursuing your life mission. If you gave away control over your life, that was *your* choice. And you have the power to reclaim that control.

If both partners in the marriage mind their own business, the union will stay happy and alive. In other words, if each takes responsibility for following their own path toward fulfilling their mission, each will feel happy and satisfied. And when you have two happy, satisfied people married to one another, you have a happy marriage!

Blaming your spouse is a waste of precious time and energy. Focus on clarifying your inner vision, and then affirming, "I can do it!" The rest will fall into place. If you're married to a healthy person, he or she will naturally be attracted to the vitality and energy you will begin to exude. This person will want to be part of your positive journey, and at that point, you can encourage your loved one to discover the inner vision deep inside.

If, like I was, you're currently married to a person who feels threatened by your happiness, you may have to consider your options. In fact, let me encourage you right now to use caution when choosing your companions—whether they be lovers, friends, co-workers, or family members. The people you associate with on a regular basis can have a tremendous positive or negative influence on you. Being around negative people who are always echoing "What's the use?" or "Dream on; we'll never have a good life like those other people," or "You're always going to be a loser," has a hypnotic effect. Their negative affirmations prevent your unconscious from believing that you have the right and the strength to succeed.

If you must spend time with negative people—for example, family members whom you simply can't avoid at times—keep these interactions to a minimum. Arm yourself with positive affirmations, and slip into the rest room often to review them and renew your positive spirit. If you had to walk into a hospital ward filled with people who had contagious diseases, you'd wear a protective mask and gown, right? It's the same situation here— only the contagious disease is negative thinking.

Your inner self will always guide you in the right direction, telling you what to do when faced with monumental decisions such as divorcing a spouse, or "divorcing" a negative friend or family member. Spend as much time as you can with your inner voice and vision. If you feel confused or scared, be patient with yourself. The inner voice is clear, but it sometimes speaks quietly, and it's easily drowned out by the noise of negative thinking and fear.

Many times, overeating is a way to stay oblivious to the unhappiness within a marriage. For example:

— Every time Patrice stopped overeating, she'd get into arguments with her husband. She wondered if diet- ing was making her irritable. That can certainly happen, but in Patrice's case, her husband's constant complaining and criticizing was the source of her irritation. As long as she binged on cakes and cookies, she was numb to the pain inflicted upon her from her husband's stinging attacks. Without her "food shield," she felt the full force of his verbal slings and arrows.

Patrice's weight-loss efforts were successful only after she directly confronted the issues driving her to overeat. Instead of running from her anger, she had to get to its source through marital therapy.

Whenever we feel the urge to overeat, that's our inner voice screaming at us to listen. It demands our attention because there's something in our life that needs fixing. We overeat to "shut up" the discomfort of having to fix or change something in our lives. The pain of having to look at our negative feelings, and uncover and maybe get to their root, is difficult. It's so much easier to grab the quick fix of food and cover up that pesky voice! But we know too well what the consequences of this quick fix are: more pain.

In the long run, it's easier to just sit still and tell your inner voice, "Okay, I'm listening to you. What do you need to tell me?" Here are some ways of tapping in to your inner voice and the answers that lie waiting deep within you:

Writing

This is a way of having a conversation with yourself. I've used this method for years, and I still find it useful if I'm feeling upset and confused (which all normal humans feel from time to time). I prefer writing at my computer terminal because I can write as quickly as I think. Other people tell me that they prefer pen and paper, or even typewriters. The medium isn't important; it's the act of writing itself that is important.

The next time you feel upset, I encourage you to write about it. Just start anywhere and don't worry about punctuation, spelling, or grammar. Just let those thoughts and feelings flow, and please don't edit or censor yourself.

Taking a Walk by Yourself

Let the rhythm of your footsteps calm you and help you focus your thoughts. I also find it helpful to make myself take notice of the beautiful colors and sounds of nature, as this helps me relax. And when I'm relaxed, my creative thinking is more acute.

Listening to Your Dreams

While we're dreaming, our unconscious mind processes the events, problems, and thoughts we've encountered during the day. Like a computer, the mind compiles all of this information and then draws logical conclusions.

For example, a co-worker may be plotting to sabotage your project. The unconscious mind might not acknowledge danger signals, but the unconscious mind is honest and aware. It sees and notices a lot of important details. In this situation, it would be normal to have a bad dream about the co-worker "warning" you as to his bad intentions. If you're not in touch with your inner voice these days, your unconscious will try to warn you with a loud, disturbing nightmare. Now, the co-worker may or may not actually be plotting against you, but your unconscious is noticing warning signs that your conscious self is trying to ignore, and the way it passes on this information is through dreams and nightmares.

A good way to tap in to this unconscious well of information is to ask yourself a question right before you fall asleep. You can mentally ask something such as: "Do I start looking for a new job?" and as you sleep, your unconscious will give you the answers. It might not be a simple answer; for example, your unconscious might reply, "Yes, look for a new job, but don't tell anyone what you're doing," or "First go to college, then look for a new job."

Dreams and nightmares are allegories or metaphors. Your unconscious doesn't directly convey information; the answers are implied in symbols. If you get in the habit—immediately after you wake up—of recalling and reviewing your dreams, you'll get enough information to answer your questions. Interpreting your own dreams is easy; it's just a matter of looking for evidence supporting the answers that you already know, deep inside. When you see this evidence, it just "clicks" that, yes, here's the answer I've been looking for.

Ask yourself a question three times before falling asleep. Many people find that writing out the question, and then putting it under the pillow, is a helpful adjunct to mentally asking yourself the question.

Meditating

Mediating is nothing more than a fancy word for clearing your thoughts of worries and details, and focusing on more important things. For those of you who have tried it, consider this a reminder to reclaim this useful habit. If you haven't tried meditation, let me encourage you to do so.

Being alone, or in the company of like-minded folks, is important to successful meditating. I'm such a water baby that I find that my meditation goes best if I'm near the ocean, a lake, or even in the shower. Water makes me feel calm. For others, it's a garden, the mountains, or the desert.

Many of my clients feel better when they turn a little corner or room in their house into a getaway place or sanctuary. Everyone needs a private corner or place—even (especially?) married people, who often share a bedroom and don't have a room of their own. This little haven is where you can read, meditate, write, or daydream.

If extra space is a problem, then consider putting a little desk in a corner, tucked away from distractions such as the television or telephone. Make the desk reflect your tastes and personality—putting things on it such as a plant, a vase of flowers, drawing paper, favorite books, or photos of happy times.

This private place is one more way of being good to yourself—a way to replace your pounds of pain with health and happiness!

chapter four

"STOP THE WORLD, I WANT TO GET OFF!": STRESS AND STRESS EATING

"Suffering ceases to be suffering in some way at the moment it finds a meaning."
— Viktor Frankl (psychiatrist who survived a Nazi concentration camp and wrote about his experiences in *Man's Search for Meaning*)

Abuse survivors who don't deal with their closeted anger and self-blame often enter into emotionally abusive adulthood situations at work or in their love lives. Abuse survivors may pride themselves on being exceptionally strong and able to withstand tremendous adversity, but the price of enduring such pain is enormous.

Those who grow up in a warm, loving environment devoid of neglect or abuse won't stand for abuse as an adult. If they find that their work setting is unbearable, they have no choice but to look for other work. Abuse survivors who attempt to endure adulthood abuse (in a marriage or job, for example) will also show symptoms of discontent, such as weight gain and health problems. But the abuse survivor blocks out awareness of this bodily feedback. She denies it and downplays how bad it is.

There's a difference between stressful situations and abusive situations. Stress, like abuse, commonly leads to overeating. The difference between the two is subtle but significant:

- Stress is unavoidable, while abuse is avoidable.

- Stress doesn't mean that your personal rights are being violated, but abuse does.

- Stressful situations can actually increase your self-esteem and strength, while abuse tears you down.

- To combat stress eating, you need to take personal measures and make personal changes; while to combat abuse, you need to remove yourself from the abuser.

The Co-ed's Weight Gain

If you were raised in a warm, nurturing family, you may have been shielded from stress until adolescence or early adulthood. That sudden shock of diving into the cold water of life sometimes catches the young adult unprepared for the challenges of independent living. And that first brush with stress can mean a first brush with out-of-control weight gain and overeating.

I've worked with a number of women who complained that they never had a weight problem until they moved away from home and went to college. This happened to Grace when she turned 18 and left home to attend a prestigious university 150 miles away. She'd had to work hard to be accepted to this competitive school, and she was determined to be at the head of the class, as she had been in high school.

Grace's Story

Grace soon discovered that she'd gone from being the big fish in a small pond, to a small fish in a big pond. "College was so much harder than I expected!" she recalled. "I had to study all the time just to keep a B average." In high school, she'd breezed through her courses.

Grace's academic pressures were compounded by her loneliness. She missed her parents, her sister, her boyfriend, and her other friends. Grace found it difficult to socialize with the seemingly sophisticated college kids, and with her studying schedule, she had little time for leisure or recreation.

All of this stress triggered an enormous appetite for food that Grace had never before experienced. The dorm food was high-fat: pizzas, cheeseburgers, and french fries. It tasted delicious to Grace's empty stomach and soul. She ate more than normal, ingested a higher fat content than normal, and exercised less than she used to. All of that added up to 25 extra pounds on her 5'5" frame. She felt fat, which further added to her shyness.

Clearly, Grace wasn't being abused. She'd come from a loving family and had never acted out addictively before. I did find a history of alcoholism in parts of Grace's family (not her parents), so she may have had some genetic predispositions to bingeing on food or alcohol. Sometimes, people with genetic predispositions have a dormant predilection for acting out addictively. Until they're confronted with abuse or undue stress, these tendencies won't be triggered. In Grace's case, she met with overwhelming stress for the first time at age 18.

And without any outlet for these troubling emotions—such as emotional support or exercise—she began overeating to ease her pain.

"I Can't Stand My Job!"

I've worked with people who were dealing with job stress, as well as those in abusive job settings. Here are their stories, to further illustrate the difference between stress and abuse:

— During the Christmas season, Mandy and her co-workers were always required to work overtime to meet increased customer demand. It was exhausting and stressful to deal with the crowds for ten or twelve hours a day. Every year, Mandy would gain ten or more pounds because she didn't exercise and also nibbled continually on holiday treats.

This is an example of stress eating.

— Paulette's boss also wanted his employees to efficiently handle the busier-than-normal Christmas rush. Unlike Mandy's situation, though, Paulette's boss would make his demands known in an abusive fashion. He'd scream at them to work faster, often using belittling and foul language. He'd call them at home and bully them into answering bizarre questions. Despite Paulette's deeply held religious beliefs, her boss insisted that she miss church and work on Sundays. He threatened to fire anyone who didn't obey his every command.

This is an example of overeating stemming from abuse.

— Marcia worked for a defense contractor. During the 1980s, thousands of workers had been hired to work on the company's lucrative military contracts. After the end of the Cold War, the company's production practically ceased. Marcia knew that 3,500 workers were due to be laid off during the coming two years. Every morning she'd wake up wondering: "Is this the day I lose my job?" She'd watch as her co-workers were laid off, one by one. The stress of waiting was unbearable, and she soon began eating huge lunches and fattening snacks. This is also stress eating.

— Another stress eater was Joel, who'd been a policeman for five years. The constant danger made Joel feel tense and on edge, and he'd wind down at night with potato chips, popcorn, or pretzels.

— Kelly's stress resulted from working at a job that didn't mesh with her personality. She was an energetic, creative person who enjoyed working on independent projects. So why was she working as an insurance claims adjuster? Because it had been the first job offered to her out of college, and she'd snapped it up. Now Kelly was miserable, feeling smothered by the enormous paper-work and huge insurance system.

Although she was competent at her job, she felt deadened by the monotony. I asked her one day why she didn't look for different work and was surprised by her reply: "In only 14 years, I can retire." I don't know about you, but to me, 14 years is an awfully long time to be miserable. Since it was impractical for Kelly to quit her job in the uncertain economy, we worked on ways to improve her job conditions and resultant satisfaction. Kelly learned to focus on the parts of her job that were somewhat creative and satisfying, such as calming people down and helping them recover from losses.

Most people, like Kelly, deal with job stress by making changes in their attitudes or work environment. In the second half of this book, you'll read about ways to deal with stress, even on the job. If you have an abusive boss or co-worker, however, the problem needs to be dealt with head-on. Ignoring abuse doesn't work. Removing yourself from the abusive situation is the only solution, either by transferring to another department, finding another job, or taking steps to have the abusive person punished or removed. None of these steps is easy. And with economic uncertainty, most of us are reluctant to rock the boat. But if an abusive job situation is negatively affecting your weight and other parts of your health, do you have any choice but to listen to your body and confront the problem?

Of course, obesity attracts additional pain. Unfortunately, many people act cruel toward those who are different from the norm, and obese people are objects of incredibly insensitive actions. People who would never poke fun at a member of a racial minority or at a disabled person don't even hesitate to call an obese person "Fatso," or some other disparaging remark.

A Harvard University study conducted from 1981 to 1988 found that 20 percent of overweight women were more likely to be unmarried, have less education, and earn an average of $6,710 less a year than thinner women. The study also found that 11 percent of overweight men were more likely to be unmarried and earn about $3,000 less a year than thinner men. It can be argued that being unmarried is not necessarily the problem. After all, some people prefer to be single. I believe these overweight people suffered sexual traumas that make them avoid, or even sabotage, long-term relationships and marriage.

Clearly, though, a number of well-constructed studies have pointed to employment discrimination toward overweight people. This is just one objective indicator of what every overweight person knows too well: Society blames you, even hates you, if you're fat.

I know from firsthand experience that when I would gain just a little weight—let's say, 20 pounds—people would treat me differently. Men would no longer open doors for me or ask me for dates. I became invisible.

This mistreatment leads to more isolation, loneliness, and other feelings that trigger eating binges. If you're depressed because you were teased and taunted, how are you going to ease your pain? With food, of course. If you're angry because nothing in your closet fits on your ever-growing body, how are you going to calm down? By eating, of course.

The Pain of Loss and Grieving

Losing a loved one is never easy. The grief that is triggered by missing someone is mixed with other painful feelings: Was it my fault? Could I have prevented this somehow? Why did this have to happen?

The process of grieving was studied by noted author Elisabeth Kübler-Ross, who wrote that grief often involves shock and disbelief, followed by attempts to "bargain" with God over the loss ("I'll go to church every Sunday if only you allow her to live.") Next, the bereaved person feels anger and betrayal, either directed toward herself, toward God, toward the situation, or toward the person who left. After anger, grieving moves into depression—what we usually think of as mourning. Normally, the pain associated with the loss subsides gradually. After about six or nine months, acceptance occurs.

Many times, though, a person gets "stuck" in one of the stages of grief. Anger and depression are the most common stopping points for people who haven't come to terms with a loss. And those who are stuck in the grieving stages of anger and depression are prone to overeat.

My clients who overate due to unresolved grief had experienced a wide variety of losses:

— Suzanne had watched her mother die of a heart attack. She desperately tried to save her mom, but it was too late.

— Jim lost his right hand in an industrial accident.

— Edith's father had shot her pet dog for committing the crime of digging up the family vegetable garden. Her grief involved unresolved anger toward her father, as well as grief associated with losing her best friend, the dog. Pet loss triggers a lot of unresolved grief because many people don't openly mourn for animals—they worry that people will think they're being silly. But our relationships with animals are often as close (or closer) as they are to any human.

— Monica's emotional pain resulted from missing her grandmother terribly. Her grandma had been her role model, confidante, and best friend when she was a girl. Although her grandmother had been gone for three years, Monica missed her terribly.

— Ruby had lost custody of her little girl, and she described the emotional pain as being similar to a death.

— Phyllis's husband had left her two years before, and she still mourned the loss of her dream of an ideal marriage. Although the marriage had never been harmonious, Phyllis hung on to the resentment and anger she felt as a result of her ex-husband's sudden departure.

— Nicki had worked for the same company for 12 years and always felt that her job was secure. When the company announced a massive layoff, Nicki didn't give it a thought, so the pink slip she found in her paycheck was a huge shock. She felt like she'd been betrayed after putting in so many years of hard work. Her grief was compounded by the losses attached to her new financial woes: She had to move from her home into a less expensive apartment, and she had to trade in her pride-and-joy red sports car for a basic sedan.

The Grief Aspect of Dieting

The most difficult loss for compulsive overeaters is giving up their very close companion and comforting friend—food.

Forgoing chocolate ice cream, cheeseburgers, or whatever food gets a person through life's difficult moments feels like the death of a loved one or best friend.

I've worked with this aspect of weight loss extensively, and I've found that acknowledging this type of grief is important. The stages of grieving over the loss of overeating are exactly like those connected to other deaths. During the shock phase, you blindly agree to do anything to lose weight: buy expensive gym memberships, sign up for diet club sessions, and swear off overeating.

The anger phase of grieving is twofold: First, the dieter struggles with questions such as, "Why me? Why do I gain weight so easily? How could I have let myself get so fat? Why can't I be like my husband who can eat anything and never gain a pound?" Next, all the pent-up anger she's been holding in— and suppressing with eating binges—comes rushing to the surface. Most people call this "irritability" from dieting, and eventually they go off their diets to feel better.

The third stage of grief involves "bargaining." This means trying to negotiate with yourself, the Universe, or God to meet your preferences. The bargaining dieter tries to stretch the laws concerning physics, digestion, calorie-burning, and metabolism to fit her own needs. For example, she may tell herself, "It's okay for me to eat a lot at Sunday brunch, because tomorrow morning I'm joining the gym," or "I'll have a second helping of dinner, and then I'll skip breakfast tomorrow."

After bargaining comes depression. The dieter reaches a behavioral fork in the road at the depression stage. She may say, "What's the use? I'll always be fat!" and abandon attempts at a healthful lifestyle. Or, she may continue her diet and substitute another compulsive behavior (alcohol, shopping, flighty relationships, and smoking are common replacements) to deal with the depression.

Much depression is rooted in anger turned inward. The result is self-blame or "Shame"— the "S" in the FATS feelings leading to overeating. Food has many chemicals, textures, and properties that deliver antidepressant effects. That's why food is so seductive to the depressed person.

The final stage of grief is Acceptance. The healthy dieter who has successfully worked through the stages of grieving and has still adhered to her balanced nutrition program knows that she needs to view weight control as a lifelong endeavor, not a temporary quick fix. She accepts the reality of her body's makeup: If she eats too much, she gains weight. If she eats light and exercises, she loses weight and tones her muscles.

Acceptance means that you understand and internalize these realities—it doesn't mean that you necessarily enjoy them. To accept means to face something head-on and to take responsibility for your actions. It doesn't mean wallowing in questions such as "Why?," but rather, determining, "Okay, what can I do to make the best of this situation?"

Post-Traumatic Eating

Stress from sudden trauma also triggers overeating. After the 1994 Los Angeles earthquake, *Los Angeles Times* columnist Robin Abcarian reported how utterly unnerving it felt to feel the ground buckling beneath her. An earthquake is extremely frightening—as a California native, I've gone through many of them, including the 1989 San Francisco quake. Abcarian wrote in the *Times* that she and her friends had replaced their normally low-cal diets with high-fat, high-bulk, high-carbohydrate foods. The muffins, bacon, and cheeseburgers were filling and comforting, calming jittery nerves fueled by too many aftershocks.

Shirley's Story

My client Shirley reacted the same way to a sudden trauma. One night while driving home from a class, her car impacted something with a loud, stomach-turning thud that could only mean one thing. She stopped the car, praying that she hadn't hit someone. But no such luck.

Another driver called an ambulance, and Shirley was so busy attending to the bicyclist she'd just hit that she didn't even notice that her nose had been broken when her face impacted the steering wheel. The bicyclist died the next day, and Shirley started psychotherapy two weeks later.

With her conscience eating away at her, Shirley started eating away at food to compensate. Her heart hurt, her nose hurt, and her body felt painfully swollen as a result of the ten pounds she'd just put on. She was haunted by recollections of the accident, barely sleeping due to recurring nightmares.

Post-traumatic stress disorder is a coping mechanism. The body throws a switch in response to sudden and overwhelming fear, a switch that alters the behavior and emotions. Insecurity, obtrusive thoughts, worry, and nightmares cloud the lives of trauma survivors, and they turn to food to feel better.

In the chapters that follow, I'll discuss some of the biological reasons why we overeat in response to trauma and stress. You'll also read about ways to replace overeating with healthier, more effective, coping measures.

Picking on Yourself

Sometimes abuse is self-inflicted, as opposed to being perpetrated by another party. Many of my clients with low self-esteem didn't feel that they deserved good. They denied themselves basic necessities, behaving like stingy parents who were neglecting their own selves.

— Although she and her husband were financially comfortable, Mindy wouldn't spend much money on clothes for herself. She always bought her children and husband top-quality shoes, clothes, and undergarments. Yet, Mindy dressed in dime-store housedresses and cheap vinyl shoes. I asked about the condition of her bras, panties, and socks; and Mindy reluctantly admitted they were worn, faded, and ill-fitting. I literally had to assign Mindy the task of purchasing new underwear, clothing, and shoes for herself. The transformation in her self-esteem was immediately apparent.

— Judy had a self-destructive habit bordering on obsessive-compulsive behavior: She constantly picked at her face. She'd squeeze pimples and blackheads and gouge chin hairs with her tweezers until her face was bleeding. Judy's complexion was always rough due to this mishandling, and she told me that her facial skin often hurt.

— Dana's life would have been so much easier if she would have simply maintained her car. Instead, she waited for things to break. As a result, she risked serious injury due to blown tires and near-failing brakes, and she was perpetually late.

— Jeannie's overeating was clearly an act of self-abuse. She desperately wanted to lose the extra 80 pounds she carried, yet she believed she wasn't capable of achieving her goals. She felt totally incompetent, and blamed herself for many things she had no control over. To punish herself for "being bad," she'd stuff herself with food until she felt nauseated by the pressure in her stomach.

Clearly, self-abuse can be deadly. Many of the sexually abused clients I worked with had attempted suicide. Many slashed their wrists and other parts of their bodies. According to Wallace (1993), a survey in *Who's Who Among American High School Students* reported that 20 percent of the nation's brightest female students said they had been sexually assaulted by someone they knew. Of those who had been sexually assaulted, 56 had experienced suicidal thoughts and 17 percent had actually attempted suicide.

Now, although not as dangerous as the examples mentioned above, low-level cumulative stress (stemming from a lot of little things) can eat away at someone after a while, too. While not serious, any form of stress that can be conquered is helpful to mention—so I'm citing some situations below that were fairly easy to overcome.

— Henrietta was disorganized and had to hunt for her keys and purse every morning, as well as pens, scissors, and other basics. So, she made a point of placing those items that she would need near the door the night before.

— Every day, Margaret struggled with an automatic garage door that almost slammed on her car as she was backing out. A call to a handyman solved a problem that had been nagging at her for months.

— Vicki kept breaking her fingernails on the rusty combination lock she used at her gym. When she finally replaced the lock for a mere five dollars, she eased that annoyance.

— Melissa was chronically late returning library books, and was always shelling out 10, 12, or 15 dollars in late fees. Part of the problem was the library's location being ten miles across town from her office and home. Melissa decided it was more economical, and less stressful, to purchase her reading material instead of borrowing it.

— Anita hadn't balanced her checkbook in over a year, and she had no idea how much money she had available to spend. She bounced checks often, and the overdraft charges of $15 were eating away at her meager savings. So she decided to open up a new account and keep careful records of her assets and debits.

— Leigh's finances were also out of control, but her situation stemmed from excessive credit card charging.

Her "cure" was to cut up her cards and pay off her balances as quickly as possible.

Self-Imposed Stress and Self-Esteem

All of the clients cited in the examples above had suffered from lowered self-esteem before they inflicted their self-imposed abuse. But clearly, by not taking care of themselves, their self-esteem had little chance of being raised.

In the case of someone who's very disorganized, this habit is one that can be deeply ingrained from the time of childhood. Other times, the person becomes increasingly accustomed to denying herself anything positive.

I particularly witnessed this phenomenon when I became aware of the buying habits of these women. No matter what, they never bought anything for themselves unless it was on sale. It didn't matter if there were two identical items, priced exactly the same. If one had a price tag that said it was marked down, that's the one they'd buy. They didn't feel that they deserved, or had the right to possess, a full-priced item.

Sometimes my clients were afraid to tell their husbands that they'd purchased something. Diana would hang her clothing purchases in the deep recesses of her closet for at least two months before wearing them. Then, if her husband noticed her wearing a new dress or blouse, she could truthfully say she'd had it for "months."

This type of sneaking around also eats away at self-esteem.

Many of my clients also implied that they didn't think they deserved to take good care of themselves until they lost weight. This is convoluted thinking, I'd explain to them. First, you take good care of yourself, then your self-esteem goes up. When your self-esteem is raised, your appetite and weight go down.

You must take good care of yourself even if you believe that you don't deserve it. "Act" as if you have high self-esteem. Pretend you're someone you admire, such as a famous movie star. Make believe that you're a thin person. Then behave in the way that you envision that person acting. Your self-esteem will catch up to your self-loving behavior.

Deep inside, your inner child will be happy that you're taking good care of her. She'll think, *Gee I must be a special little girl to deserve such good treatment.* And when the little girl inside of you feels good about herself, it's reflected in the way that *you* feel about yourself.

Consider this: You like to be around people who treat you well, don't you? People who say nice things to you and who consider your needs and feelings? And, conversely, wouldn't you rather avoid people who say mean things to you and who are selfish? Well, you can have the same relationship priorities with your own self. If you're good to yourself, you'll be happier and more comfortable. If you neglect yourself, you'll feel unloved and lonely.

The point to remember is: First, be good to yourself. *Then* you'll lose weight.

chapter five

PLAYING DOCTOR
ISN'T CHILD'S PLAY

"I have never begun any important venture for which I felt adequately prepared."
— Dr. Sheldon Kopp,
author of *Raise Your Right Hand Against Fear*

Stephanie, a 33-year-old legal secretary, was crying as she sat in my office. "My husband says our sex life isn't good enough for him," she said, blinking her tear-stained blue eyes. "I know what the problem is. It's because I'm too fat!" She sobbed uncontrollably into her tissue, repeating how unattractive she felt, bemoaning the fact that her overweight body was the root of all her unhappiness. The truth, of course, was the reverse: Her unhappiness, including the problems with her sex life, precipitated the fat on her body.

I requested that she bring her husband, Raymond, with her for the next therapy session. She did so, and although Raymond seemed uncomfortable at first, after listening to Stephanie for a while, he opened up in an impassioned manner.

"Stephanie, your body has nothing to do with our problems!" he told her emphatically. "I wouldn't mind if you'd lose some weight, but the main problem is that you never want sex. And when we finally do make love, you seem to be completely turned off. It's like your body's there, but your heart's not into it at all. How am I supposed to be turned on if you're not turned on, too?"

Stephanie looked shocked by her husband's protestations. She almost couldn't believe that her husband really wasn't turned off by her cellulite and soft rolls of fat.

Once Stephanie understood Raymond's position—that he wanted his wife to fully participate in their sex life—they were on the road to healing. I worked with the couple to help them communicate their desires and fears within the relationship, and we also discussed ways of heightening sexual pleasure for both of them.

I worked closely with Stephanie to discover the root of her inability to *enjoy* making love. It turned out that Stephanie needed to give herself permission to relax and enjoy sex. Her early experiences, we discovered, had taught her that sex was dirty and wrong.

Stephanie's Story

At the time of her first sexual experience, Stephanie was five years old, a cute wide-eyed brunette with a big smile. Her older brother, Bob, had taken her to a neighbor's house on one of those Saturday mornings when time stretches out endlessly for children. At the house, the parents were gone for the day, leaving their three sons home alone. This also meant that Stephanie was alone with four preadolescent males—a combustible situation.

As if they had planned it, one of the neighbor boys asked Bob to practice hoopshots in the backyard with him. This left Stephanie alone with the other two boys, Tony and David, who asked her if she wanted to "play doctor." The little girl, not knowing any better, said okay. She would be the patient, the boys said, and they would be the two doctors.

"First, you take off all your clothes," said Tony. Stephanie complied, too young to be controlled by modesty impulses. Once she was naked, Tony told her to lie down on the bed. "Okay, pretend you're really sick, and we'll take care of you."

The boys—overwhelmed by curiosity and never before having seen a naked girl—ran their hands all over her body. They paid very close attention to Stephanie's genitals, spreading her legs and exploring her labia and vaginal opening. Stephanie was eager to comply and didn't protest, except when David stuck his finger into her vagina.

"Ouch!" she yelped, "You're hurting me!"

"Just relax," David forcefully told her. "Remember, we're doctors and we have to do this." Stephanie closed her eyes tightly and put her hands flat against her hips to brace herself against the pain. Tears rolled down her eyes as Tony and David continued exploring her genitals.

"Hey, what are you doing!?" The bedroom door slammed open as Bob and his friend returned from playing basketball. Bob glared at Tony and David, and their brother was yelling at the two younger boys.

"Get dressed. Let's get out of here, Steph!" Bob ordered his little sister. She struggled to pull up her little pants and grimaced at the pain when the fabric touched her tender genitals. Stephanie walked gingerly downstairs as Bob urged her to exit quickly.

Bob and Stephanie told their parents everything that had happened, expecting the adults to intervene by admonishing the neighbors. Instead, Bob and Stephanie were both spanked—hard—for their "foolishness." Confused and humiliated, Stephanie's views on sexuality had just been formed.

So it was no wonder that Stephanie avoided sex. She had always associated the act with pain, exploitation, and punishment.

The Myth of Playing Doctor

Many "child-care experts" dismiss childhood sexual exploration as harmless, since sexual curiosity is normal and natural. While curiosity *is* natural for children, and this inquisitiveness often leads to the exploration of male/female differences, "playing doctor" is not a harmless avenue. Too many girls and boys, such as Stephanie, are victimized at the hands of older children. David and Tony ignored Stephanie's cries and protestations and used her body to satisfy themselves. They crossed the line into abuse, because they got carried away and didn't care about Stephanie.

Harmless sexual exploration does exist, of course. Prepubescent boys look at their own genitals and masturbate. Little girls marvel at the sensations of their labia and clitoris touching a bicycle seat or horse's back. And same-sex exploration is extremely common among both sexes. In fact, I've had a number of clients come to terms with fears that they were homosexual, when all they had been doing as children was exploring their newly discovered sexuality.

— For example, Kathleen and her four close girl-hood friends had touched each other's naked breasts and labia during slumber parties. For years, Kathleen kept this a closely guarded secret, feeling she'd committed some horrible "crime." When she learned, in therapy, that her experience was fairly common among young people, she was greatly relieved.

— Jerry had similar fears about the mutual mastur-bation sessions he and his best friend, Brian, had engaged in during one summer vacation. They'd taken turns holding each other's penises and "jerking each other off" until ejaculating. At the time, it had been a powerful sexual experience that they both greatly enjoyed and laughed about. Over the years, though—especially since his relationships with women weren't working very well— Jerry harbored secret fears that he might be gay. Like Kathleen, Jerry was relieved to dis-cover that his childhood experiences were quite normal.

The line between normal sexual exploration and sexual abuse is crossed as soon as one person is not a voluntary participant. The child who is pressured, coerced, tricked, forced, or manipu-lated is the one who suffers the emotional consequences of an abuse survivor. It is those emotions, not the actual physical sexu-al act, that cause the harm and confusion.

That's why "playing doctor" can be just as emotionally harm-ful to children as full-on intercourse. The physical manifestation of sexual abuse can take any form, but if the child is flooded with feelings too powerful to handle or understand, the girl or boy is emotionally injured.

The Pound/Pain Link

Today, many people have become aware of the emotional reasons behind overeating. We overeat because of stress, anger, fatigue, depression, loneliness, and insecurity. However, abuse survivors overeat without conscious awareness that they have any choice over eating. Abuse survivors, in other words, feel *compelled* to overeat. They literally eat like there's no tomorrow because, for the abused, "tomorrow" is an abstract concept. The past, instead, rules their lives.

Playing doctor in abusive ways makes children ripe for eating disorders. Take Becky, for example.

Becky's Story

Becky was six years old when her older stepbrother, Michael, locked her in the bathroom and convinced her to take a shower with him. He seductively soaped Becky's body and spent way too much time lathering her genitals with his hands.

Becky was frightened. She was afraid that Michael would reject her if she protested. She was afraid her parents would disapprove—or worse. She was also afraid because the situation just felt wrong. Yet, at the same time, she was aware of pleasurable sensations induced by the soap, warm water and Michael's fingers stroking her vaginal opening.

But her pleasure was short-lived when, after the shower, Michael grabbed Becky's shoulders, shook her hard, and warned in a menacing voice, "Don't you ever tell Mom and Dad we took a shower together. If you do, they'll have a big fight and probably get a divorce. And it will be *your* fault!"

Becky, at age six, had just learned that pleasure and fear were interrelated. This process, whereby humans and animals can be changed after one powerful emotional experience is called "one-trial learning." For example, if a balloon pops loudly near your dog, he may, from that point onward, react with fear to the sound of balloons. Someone who eats a bad piece of fish and gets violently ill may feel nauseated by the smell of cooking fish, even for years after the original experience occurred.

In Becky's case, she experienced two powerful sensations simultaneously—sexual arousal and intense fear—and she linked the two together. As Becky grew up, her relationships with boys were affected by this one-trial learning experience. When she was 14 and kissed a boy for the first time, the sexual arousal she felt scared her to the point where she avoided this boy forever. When she got married, Becky avoided sex as much as possible.

Our sexuality is also deeply linked to our self-image. We all have private, inner lives and feelings about who we are, deep inside ourselves. Our sexuality is a bridge between our inner, private selves and our public selves. Sex is something deeply personal, yet it is also something we share with certain people.

Our first sexual experiences often set the tone for how we view the other private parts of ourselves. If we have a negative initial sexual experience—as Becky did—we internalize this negativity and apply those feelings of fear, shame, and anger to ourselves. Becky had every right to be furious with her stepbrother, but she was too young to know who was truly responsible for their ill-advised shower. Before the age of ten, children see themselves as the center of the universe—everything revolves around them. So, naturally, this shower experience must have been Becky's fault.

Becky experienced deep fear and insecurity after the shower, not to mention that she also felt defective. She was intensely ashamed by her feelings of sexual arousal, and she was convinced that she was the only person to ever have those sensations. She had nightmares about adults touching her genitals, and during those dreams, Becky was sexually aroused. Then she'd wake up in a cold sweat. Normally, Becky would cry out to her mother after a nightmare, but now she was too frightened to tell anyone about her bad dreams.

Instead, Becky turned to food for solace. She was especially fond of peanut butter and jelly sandwiches, which comforted her when she did her homework alone in her room at night. The extra-crunchy peanut butter and crisp toasted bread helped ease the fear and anxiety that was buried so deeply below the surface that Becky actually began to think that it was normal to feel afraid and insecure. As long as she was eating, Becky felt okay about herself.

While Becky was never obese as an adult, she constantly carried 25 extra pounds on her 5'5" body. The sandwiches kept Becky's sexual arousal level, fears, and insecurities out of conscious awareness. She also avoided attracting much male sexual attention by staying slightly plump and then by dressing unattractively.

Anytime a man looked her way, Becky would catch her breath and feel flushed with mild anxiety.

Healing the Pound/Pain Link

Becky, as well as other "playing doctor" survivors, turned to food out of necessity, since little girls have few emotional anesthetics available to them. If the trauma had occurred during adulthood, Becky could have chosen from adult-type outlets, some healthy, some not. She could have shopped, jogged, seen a therapist, gotten drunk, smoked pot, argued with her husband, yelled at her children, driven her car fast, written in her journal, or called her best friend. But all Becky had, at age six, was food. She was too ashamed to talk to her mother about her experiences, and she certainly couldn't talk to her stepbrother. She didn't know about organized forms of physical exercise, and she was too young to go shopping or call someone. So she ate.

Growing up, Becky repressed the memories of that unpleasant shower episode. Occasionally, the incident would pop up in her mind, but she would immediately dismiss it as something minor and insignificant. When she started therapy as an adult, Becky told the therapist that she'd had a "perfect childhood" with "no abuse at all." Becky had actually convinced herself that the incident had had no bearing on her self-image.

Having worked with abuse survivors over the years, I've seen this type of scenario again and again. The original hurtful situation is a faint, recurring memory disregarded as inconsequential. So, in light of the information that has been presented up to this point, here's the first step in breaking the pound/pain link:

1. Know your history.

If a memory resurfaces once or twice a month, that memory is trying to tell you something. Think of the memory as a teacher who has something for you to learn. Although it may be frightening or painful to learn that teacher's lesson, in the long run, life will be calmer and make more sense. In other words, it's worth taking the time and effort to listen to your inner teacher.

Is there a faint, distant memory that pops up in your mind periodically? I'm not asking you to create one, but instead, to be aware of what's already there. Whenever I would ask a client this question, they would quickly downplay the importance of their recurring memory. That tendency stemmed from the fact that the person had lived with the memory for so long that it had been integrated into their internal landscape. It was a familiar scene, and that familiarity caused it to be dismissed as ordinary and insignificant.

However, as soon as the recurring memory was discussed in therapy, the client would instantly recognize how powerful the emotions behind the memory still were. And that takes us to Step 2 in your healing process:

2. Write a one- or two-sentence description of your memory.

At this point, you needn't elaborate on your original hurtful situation. You just need to recategorize it, from a seemingly fictitious and faded memory, to a significant piece of your personal history. In other words, you need to make the memory real.

If you write down a very brief description of your memory, it will stop haunting you. Even if you're not really sure what happened—and even if you're not sure it *actually* happened—write down the memory. We're not going to make a big deal out of this memory, or make it something more than it was. We're simply going to listen to it.

3. Be aware of the emotions accompanying the memory.

As you write down this memory, pay attention to any emotional reactions you may have. Do you feel nervous, tense, or anxious at all? Are your teeth clenched, or are your fists rolled together? Is your heart pounding? Do you feel lightheaded or dizzy? Or do you have doubts about the credibility of the memory and wonder whether writing it down might be opening a "can of worms"? These are all common emotions you can expect to feel when the recurring memory is nailed down on paper.

Another reaction might be your desire to put this book aside for a while to avoid dealing with the subject. Other people might find their appetite for food increases as they recall these memories, with the added frustration that they're temporarily overeating while reading this book. But, in the long run, by becoming more aware of how normal these reactions are, you can progress on your path toward serenity and a normal body weight.

You see, your food cravings and increased appetite serve as teachers in the same respect that your recurring memory is a teacher. There are important lessons inherent in these situations, and until the lessons are digested, the teachers won't go away. Instead of getting angry at yourself for eating all the time, this could be the point where you begin to take a different approach to your overactive appetite. Instead of wrestling with your appetite or being controlled by it, you might discover why it's so large to begin with.

The first part of healing occurs in the mind. The second part occurs in the heart. The third and final part of healing occurs in the stomach. Initially, you need to achieve an intellectual understanding of the painful situations triggering the need to overeat. Then, the next step is to acknowledge and release the powerful emotions attached to the situations. When that happens, the stomach reacts by triggering the return to a normal appetite for food. Our appetite will no longer need our attention because we will have learned its lessons. We won't *need* to be hungry anymore.

Keep going!

chapter six

UNWANTED ADVANCES—
PSYCHOLOGICAL SEXUAL ABUSE

"Believe that life is worth living and your
belief will help create the fact."
— William James

A strangely sad occurrence often happens during early adolescence. Young girls' self-esteem levels drop markedly, at
about the same time that their breasts and sexuality begin to
develop. As far as I'm concerned, there is a direct cause-and-
effect relationship between these two milestones—that is, the
emerging sexual attractiveness and lowered self-esteem in girls.

When males first pay sexual attention to a girl, it can be both
confusing and frightening. Parents and teachers rarely prepare an
adolescent or preadolescent for this turn of events, and girls often
have no idea how to react to such a situation.

I remember the first time a man whistled at me. I was riding
my Stingray bicycle at age 12. My breasts had just begun to
develop—no more than little mounds that wouldn't fit into the
teeniest training bra, but breasts nonetheless. I was a little girl
with an emerging woman's body and very little awareness of the
complexity of male/female relationships.

When I heard the unmistakable wolf whistle, I turned my head to see who was being whistled at. I expected to see, well, a woman. Instead, I saw a man driving a Ford Mustang with his head hanging out the window and his eyes on *me*. *Why would a man whistle at me, a little girl of average attractiveness,* I remember thinking. There must be some mistake. But after that first time, it kept happening. Men and boys were noticing me, and I didn't know how to handle it.

Why didn't I talk to my mother about this new development in my life? Looking back, I guess the attention I was receiving from men really wasn't that big of a deal to me. Plus, the frequency of wolf whistles and other signs of male attention happened so gradually that eventually I got used to it. It's an awkward situation, to say the least. On the one hand, females enjoy the attention and approval. On the other hand, the attention can be embarrassing, since many young girls don't know how to react to it. Do we smile, or does this encourage the man? Do we ignore him, or does this make us look stuck-up? Do we flip the man the bird, or does this make us look like a bitch?

Isn't it complicated being a woman?

The type of harmless flirting mentioned above is fairly innocent in nature, with the most serious result being embarrassment on the part of the female. In some cases, flirting can actually be pleasant and uplifting, if the man involved is sincere. The best "pickup line" I ever received was when a man came up to me at the grocery store and gushed, "I can't *believe* there's not a wedding ring on that finger of yours!" Harmless stuff, that type of flirting.

However, flirting crosses the line into abuse when one of the following situations occurs:

1. There is psychological sexual abuse. This occurs when an inappropriate adult—your father,

stepfather, boss, uncle, doctor, and so on—relates to you in a sexual manner.

2. There are implicit put-downs in the flirting. For example, if someone implies you are "cheap," "easy," promiscuous or "slutty," that's not flirtation—that's an insult and could constitute abuse.

3. Inappropriate sexual touching is involved.

We'll explore all three situations in this chapter, as well as come to understand how they're linked to overeating. Later on in the book, we'll discuss ways to heal the pound/pain link so that your appetite and body weight can both return to normal.

Psychological Sexual Abuse

I've counseled numerous clients who were scarred—not by physical sexual assaults—but by psychological ones. And of the two, the psychological sexual abuse cases often make the deepest impact. The subtle, almost intangible nature of this form of abuse leaves the victim feeling like she's trying to hold on to a cloud or a mirage. She knows there's something there, but she can't quite put her finger on it.

Don't get me wrong. Victims of rape or incest have an enormous amount of baggage to contend with, as we'll see in subsequent chapters. But survivors of psychological sexual abuse tend to wrestle with the struggling notion that, "Well, nothing that bad really happened to me." They constantly deny and dismiss their painful memories.

Psychological sexual abuse takes on many forms. Some of the stories that follow—as experienced by my clients over the years—illustrate the many different ways in which this life-altering situation can manifest itself.

— Brenda grew up in a house where sexually explicit material was openly displayed. Everything from soft-core pornographic magazines to X-rated books and sex-paraphernalia catalogs were strewn on the living room coffee table. Brenda would browse through the material when her parents weren't around, and although she didn't fully understand what she was looking at, this material did shape her feelings with respect to how a woman was supposed to look and behave.

At night, when her parents would watch X-rated movies on television, Brenda would crouch by the staircase and watch. As an adult, Brenda could never shake the deep-seated feeling that sex was dirty, a way of thinking that interfered with her marital relationship. She see-sawed between voraciously craving food and struggling to achieve the body dimensions of a magazine center-fold—two desires that manifested themselves in a severe case of bulimia.

— Teresa's father and stepmother thought they were doing her a favor by being very open about sexuality. Both adults walked around the house naked, and Teresa was encouraged to shower with them. Not only that, but her parents openly made love in front of Teresa, thinking that if she was exposed to sex at a young age, she'd grow up thinking that it was a normal, beautiful act. Not surprisingly, though, her parents' behavior during intercourse frightened her.

That fear remained with Teresa as she grew into adulthood, and every time she made love, the image of her parents' heaving, naked bodies entered her mind and disgusted her. Needless to say, this reaction interfered with Teresa's relationships, and at age 46 she was worried that she'd never get married. Her closest relationship was with food.

— Marcia's parents divorced when she was three, and she was raised by her beautiful young mother, who brought a succession of boyfriends home while Marcia was growing up. During her formative years, Marcia received a lot of advice from her mother with respect to men and dating—advice offered way too prematurely, given Marcia's age. Her mother was determined to groom Marcia to marry well, so she dressed the little girl in extremely seductive and sexually provocative outfits. She encouraged Marcia to wiggle her hips and wear makeup. "It's never too early to start," was her mother's motto, but in truth, it was way too early.

Marcia grew up thinking herself as an object, destined to be used for men's pleasure. She didn't learn how to listen to her own inner desires and voice, and really had no idea what she wanted. Marcia only knew what men wanted and what her mother wanted. She was entirely outer-directed and gave the appearance of being a superficial, insincere people pleaser.

Deep inside, Marcia's soul was screaming for acknowledgment and attention. In therapy, Marcia learned to attend to her own needs and how to balance taking care of others with taking care of herself. She had drowned out her soul's piteous cries with alcohol and food (she never binged, but she did snack all day long). However, as soon as she started paying attention to her own needs, Marcia's cravings for food and alcohol diminished.

— Like Marcia, Suzanne was raised by a single mother who regularly brought dates home. Growing up, Suzanne heard a lot of sexual sounds emanating from the bedroom, without having the maturity to understand what she was hearing.

"I can still hear my mom screaming, 'Oh God, oh God!'" Suzanne recalled. "To this day, I am totally silent when I make love with my husband, and I know it's because I don't want to be loud like my mom." Suzanne learned to fill up the silence with large amounts of food.

— Karen was also privy to inappropriate sexual material growing up, but not the muffled panting and cries of intercourse. Instead, Karen was subjected to dirty jokes told by her father and uncle during their weekend-afternoon drinking marathons. The men would insist that Karen listen in as they reeled off their lewd tales.

"I guess they thought it was cute to watch a little girl's face turn red or get contorted when they would tell these horrible jokes," Karen painfully recounted. "Sometimes they would even ask me to memorize and repeat these jokes when friends would drop by. Everyone would get such a laugh out of it, but I was always so mad at my dad for forcing me to hear and say these awful things. It was gross!"

Karen's anger and feelings of helplessness were compounded by the fact that her mother didn't attempt to "rescue" her from the clutches of her father's sick humor. The joke's content also made Karen form a low opinion of herself as she grew up. "Thanks to my dad, I assumed that men thought of women as sex objects," she recalled. "So, I never pursued any relationships because I didn't want to be just some guy's 'hole,' as my dad would refer to women."

Karen's weight topped 200 pounds before she reached age 21. Her father would joke about her weight and her extra-large breasts and buttocks. "I hid the hurt as best I could," Karen remembered with tears burning her eyes. "But as soon as I had the opportunity, I'd eat to feel better."

— Deborah's mother, Anne, was a self-admitted flirt. At 43, Anne still thought of herself as attractive, but she actively sought male attention to bolster her aging ego. When Deborah started dating at age 15, Anne would flirt with her daughter's boyfriends. "At first I thought I was imagining it," remembered Deborah, "but after a while I saw how my Mom would dress really sexy whenever my boyfriend was supposed to come over. He even remarked once, 'Boy, you sure have a sexy Mom.' I was so embarrassed! Here, everyone else's mothers were normal housewives or working women. But my Mom thought she was Britney Spears or something!"

By competing with her daughter for male sexual attention, Anne was committing a double psychological crime. She was having a "mental affair" with her daughter's boyfriend, and she was also teaching her daughter unhealthy ways to relate to other women. Even today, Deborah has difficulty trusting other women.

Deborah also internalized her mother's behavior in a way that negatively affected her own self-image. She negatively compared herself to Anne and other attractive women, believing she was "less than" they were. Deborah also mistrusted herself, a product of the way she felt about her mother while growing up.

Deborah, too, tried to suppress her pain through food. She was so sure that she was undesirable and unattractive that she didn't even try to maintain her looks or health through proper nutrition or exercise. "Why try?" was her motto.

— Kristy was also psychologically sexually abused by her mother. At age 12, Kristy began developing large breasts, like her mom, and soon after, she started her period. That's when Kristy's mother had "a talk" with her.

"My mom told me how dirty and awful sex was," Kristy explained. "She said that guys are only interested in one thing, and I must never ever give in until marriage. I mean, she went on and on about how sex was this horrible duty you had to perform for your husband."

When Kristy asked her mother for a training bra; and permission to shave the coarse, dark hair on her legs, her mother reacted violently. "She slapped me!" said Kristy. "She said only sluts shaved their legs and wore bras. When I protested that she wore a bra and shaved her legs, she slapped me again. I never asked her another thing about sex."

Not surprisingly, Kristy became a teenage mother at age 16. Ignorant about birth control and eager to rebel against her mother, Kristy had slept with her boyfriend without using precautions. When she came to me for therapy, she was the unwed mother of three young children, and she felt angry and bitter about her life. Living in a trailer park, on welfare, the only outlet for pleasure she had was eating, and at age 30, Kristy's weight topped 250 pounds.

— Jennifer's situation was, unfortunately, extremely common. Her father paid so much attention to Jennifer's maturing body that he, essentially, psychologically molested her.

For example, her father would constantly comment on her obviously budding breasts. "It felt creepy," Jennifer remembered, "knowing that my father was constantly checking me out. I mean, he'd talk about my boobs nonstop. It was practically like incest or something!"

While a father's guidance during the sensitive adolescent transition period can, in some cases, be healthy and helpful, Jennifer's father's attentiveness triggered extreme self-consciousness in her. To conceal her breasts, she wore baggy sweaters and jackets, and if a boyfriend paid too much attention to her figure, Jennifer would scream at him.

Jennifer's subsequent obsession with dieting was a direct offshoot of her father's sexually laced attention. Both anorexics and compulsive dieters exhibit a fear of sexual attention, and they often starve themselves into asexual little-boy-like body shapes. In fact, they lose so much body fat that their breasts, hips, and menstrual cycles practically disappear.

The Abuser's Role

The adults described in the aforementioned cases acted irresponsibly toward their children. They hurt their offspring by marring their children's perspectives on relationships and healthy sexuality. As a result, they damaged their kids' self-confidence.

It's doubtful that these adults intentionally tried to hurt their children. Most abusive parents I've worked with wouldn't be considered "bad people" as such. Instead, they're oblivious, unaware, and clumsy—usually due to a mental illness, or addictions to alcohol or prescription or illegal drugs.

Later, I'll delve more deeply into the hidden anger attached to abuse, but for now, I want to emphasize that *blaming* your parents for having abused you won't serve any useful purpose. The worst thing you can do is to harbor resentment—that's a destructive emotion that will most assuredly trigger overeating episodes.

During the early stages of healing your pound/pain link, the most important thing is to *understand*—purely intellectually at this point—the source of the pain that led to your accumulation of excess weight. But not quite yet.

Keep reading: You need to take each step in your recovery as it comes.

Invisible Abuse?

Up until now in this chapter, we've focused on subtle forms of abuse. Psychological sexual abuse damages children, yet it's difficult to identify. Unlike a concrete physical act such as rape, molestation, or sodomy, the abuse described so far is almost invisible. Like a ghost, it haunts, frightens, and scars its victims.

And also like an apparition, these forms of abuse are difficult to describe and confront.

The adult abuser denies to him- or herself that a harmful act was committed. The abuser, most likely already suffering from low self-esteem, has a burning desire to be right all the time. If the abuser admits to a misdeed, the self-esteem is wounded even further.

In addition, the abuser's awareness of his or her abusive actions is often impaired by alcohol and drugs. One man I worked with had molested his daughter during an alcoholic blackout; he had no recollection of the event whatsoever. The man wasn't trying to escape responsibility for his actions— he was extremely distressed by the incident. His alcoholism had simply blocked his conscious recollection of the deplorable act.

But getting back to more tangible forms of abuse, you can probably see how its very nature might make it difficult to pinpoint clearly and definitively. Not only are the more subtle forms of psychological abuse often repressed on the part of the abuser, but, as shown through the stories in this chapter, they are repressed on the part of the victim, too. Whatever the degree of remorse on the part of the perpetrator, though, the victim still needs to deal with the pain and come to terms with it in some way.

Please don't get me wrong. I'm definitely not defending or justifying the abuser's acts. In fact, I rarely worked professionally with abusers, because their level of sickness was so great. However, those whom I have worked with were actively involved in recovery from alcoholism, drug addiction, and mental illnesses.

In any case, I do think that survivors of abuse can significantly contribute to their own healing by looking objectively at their abuser's motivations and mind-set. As you read on, you might find that this level of objectivity will help *you* explore your own emotions and help you gain control over any feelings of rage you may be experiencing. By perceiving the abuser as a very sick person with a low level of awareness, you'll be better able to reframe your abuse history in a way that will bring you peace of mind. And with it, you can achieve freedom from overeating and weight gain.

You don't need to forgive the abuser. In fact, that would be unrealistic right now. But you do need to understand what happened to you in order to be free of pain. To be finally free.

Inappropriate Touching

A more tangible form of abuse often associated with overeating later in life takes the form of "inappropriate touching." Although not as blatant as crimes such as rape or incest, Amy's case will illustrate how this sexual abuse "ghost" can still shatter children's trust and self-image.

Amy's Story

Amy was a strikingly beautiful brunette with a master's degree in chemistry. In her prestigious research position at the local university, she had achieved much success, and she'd been published in several professional journals. Yet, for all her achievements, Amy did not feel good about herself when she came in to see me for psychotherapy.

As we delved into Amy's history, some powerfully negative feelings surfaced. First, Amy acknowledged her ambivalence about her body. She always wore very masculine, boxy suits to work, ostensibly for the sake of maintaining professionalism. But in truth, Amy's fear of attracting male sexual attention made her choose the unattractive, oversized suits she wore. Even on personal trips out of town, when no colleague of Amy's could possibly see her, she wore unflattering clothing.

But her fashion choices were only the most visible symptoms of Amy's confusion with respect to her self-image. Below the surface, Amy was dealing with many more issues. First, she was intensely jealous of any woman she considered attractive, especially provocatively dressed women. Amy was so threatened by females whom she perceived in this way that she'd broken up with three boyfriends whom she'd unjustly accused of infidelity. In all three cases, Amy's insecurity had precipitated bitter, jealous fights.

"I always felt as if my boyfriends would rather be with a prettier woman," Amy recalled. She described a typical example of her jealousy-based relationship problems: She and her most recent boyfriend, Ronald, a teacher at the university, were walking around the campus on a beautiful autumn afternoon. Everything had been perfect—the weather, the scenery, the conversation. Everything, that is, until Amy spotted a curvy coed approaching the couple.

It was one of Ronald's students, who asked him a question about her homework assignment. Their conversation was brief, but Amy was red-faced with rage by the time the student walked away. She blew up at Ronald, accusing him of flirting with the girl, of having inappropriate relationships with his students. Ronald tried to defend himself, but Amy stormed off.

"And that's pretty much how most of my relation-

ships end," she said quietly. "I just get so jealous that
I blow up."

We focused on Amy's conflicting feelings with respect
to allowing herself to be attractive. She discussed her fears,
which were triggered when men flirted with her. She also
discussed her feelings associated with *being* attractive, as
well as *not being* attractive.

In my work with abuse survivors, I constantly saw
this femininity ambivalence. An offshoot of society's
madonna-whore paradox where women feel pressured to
"be virginal, but be sexy and attractive,"Amy's confusion centered on how she fit into this loop. As a professional woman in a "man's field," Amy fought to be taken
seriously, so she wore a man's uniform to disguise the
femininity that she linked with weakness.

Now, while it's true that wearing short skirts and
tight sweaters can spell professional suicide in circles
such as Amy's, she could have worn fashionable, well-
fitted suits without sacrificing the respect of her peers.

Clothing is a symbol and an indicator of self-esteem. Women
like Amy who consistently hide their bodies in too-baggy clothing often harbor deep fears of femininity and male sexual attention. Conversely, women who consistently wear too-tight,
provocative clothing may fear rejection and have a great need for
attention. Interestingly enough, women who make a habit of
wearing raggedy old bras and panties are showing a form of self-
contempt, but that's another subject.

In Amy's case, her fears about female sexuality stemmed from
an incident that occurred while she was in her teens. Although Amy
downplayed its significance at first, saying, "Oh, it just happened

once," or "I'm really making too big a deal out of nothing," the fact that she thought about it regularly signified its importance.

What happened was this: When Amy was 14, her favorite uncle, who was 29 (and very cute), was coming over to her house for a family dinner. Amy had a crush on him, and she'd looked forward to seeing him all day. She took extra care to braid her hair, and she wore the new dress she'd received at Christmas. Deep green velvet, the dress perfectly skimmed over her slim hips and budding breasts, making her look like a young beauty queen.

When Amy made her entrance into the kitchen, where her uncle was seated, the impact was enormous. He let out an appreciative whistle and said, "Amy, if you weren't my niece, I'd ask you out on a date right now." Amy's heart skipped a beat, and she blushed. She felt shy, at a loss for words.

Her uncle wasn't shy, though. In fact, the more beer he drank, the louder and bolder his flirtations became. Then it happened. After dinner, Amy was washing dishes at the sink, and her uncle came over and stood next to her, breathing his hot beer breath on her neck. She could sense impending trouble, but she didn't move away.

He proceeded to put his arm around her and kiss her on the cheek. As he kissed her, his hand dropped down to her breast, and he squeezed it, full-on, with his whole hand.

Amy dropped her dish towel and ran silently to her bedroom. She ripped off her green velvet dress and kicked it into a little ball, pushing it to the back of her closet. When she rediscovered the dress a month later, she threw it in the trash.

Amy never wore pretty dresses after that. She gradually stopped wearing anything that risked attracting male attention. In therapy, I helped Amy acknowledge the importance of what had happened to her back then. While to some teenagers, this incident might have been inconsequential, for a girl as sensitive as Amy, the situation served to paralyze her with fear and shame about being an attractive woman. As a result, she refused to allow herself to express her feminine side and tended to resent those women who could.

For Amy, the incident was anything but small.

Now, why did I include this case study here? After all, Amy did not have an eating disorder as much as she had a distorted image of herself, both physically and emotionally. Well, the reason is that this type of distortion is usually associated with women who overeat. Instead of wearing ill-fitting clothing, many women hide their femininity in mounds of extra pounds.

Inappropriate touching is a not-so-subtle form of abuse that leaves its victims feeling dirty and ashamed. They blame themselves for attracting the unwanted advance, and then proceed to downplay the situation, saying, "Maybe I just imagined that he touched me there. Maybe it was just an accident."

Whatever the rationalization, the end result is the same: A victim of inappropriate touching takes responsibility for an act that she did not bring upon herself, and instead of feeling angry at the abuser, she turns the anger inward on herself.

You'll learn how to release this type of anger in the second part of this book.

chapter seven

VIOLATED AT HOME

*"True courage is like a kite;
a contrary wind raises it higher."*
— John Petit-Senn

Incest. The word alone makes one shudder. It's horrible to think about an adult violating the trust of a child, especially a child related to the adult by blood. Yet, incest in its many forms is more common than we can imagine. Fathers, stepfathers, uncles, brothers—and even mothers, aunts, and sisters—are the perpetrators of this pernicious form of sexual abuse.

Research, and my own clinical experience, has pointed to enormous emotional and psychological transformations in children who are subject to acts of incest. Guilt and self-blame are usually integral elements of the incest survivor's pain.

Joanne's Story

When Joanne came to me for treatment, she was what those in this profession refer to as "therapy-wise." She had seen four or five other therapists before me, and had checked in and out of psychiatric hospitals. Joanne had told her story so many times that she recounted it without showing any trace of emotion.

She told me how her then 20-year-old uncle—her father's brother—would spend every summer with the family. When she was six years old, the uncle began "seducing" Joanne. First, he'd hold her on his lap. Then, he would take her in her bedroom and give her long, pleasurable back rubs. Joanne, the oldest of four siblings, loved all the attention her uncle showered on her. She even developed a little crush on him.

One day, Joanne's uncle was rubbing her back, and he asked her to take her clothes off so "he could give me an extra-special massage." Joanne gladly obliged, and that's when her uncle's fingers began exploring her genitals. Joanne haltingly described the next part: It's obvious that she was confused and conflicted about her feelings.

On the one hand, the attention was emotionally delicious to Joanne. No adult had ever been so attentive to her before. And, on a purely physical level, the back rubs were wonderful. She had opened her heart and emotions to her uncle—Joanne trusted him completely.

Then he violated that trust by touching her genitals. But Joanne ignored her natural feelings of alarm and panic and only paid attention to the pleasurable physical sensations his fingers evoked. She felt erotically aroused, even though her stomach ached with the thought that "this isn't right." At the same time, her uncle reassured Joanne that he loved her and that she was his special princess.

Every summer, the incestuous acts would escalate. By the time she was 11 years old, Joanne and her uncle were engaging in sexual intercourse on a regular basis, and she was becoming increasingly confused. On the one hand, Joanne craved her uncle's attention and love, and she even enjoyed the physical sensations of sex for the most part. But the secrecy surrounding their relationship, pounded home by her uncle's warning: "Don't you ever tell no one about us—you hear?" reminded Joanne that what they were doing was very, very wrong.

Joanne began eating in secret, as she felt more and more isolated from her family. With no one to confide in, Joanne turned to food for solace and companionship. She gained so much weight that her uncle actually rejected her as being "too fat" when he arrived for the summer of her 13th year. This rejection escalated the extent of Joanne's secret eating even more.

Clearly, Joanne's incestuous relationship had deeply penetrated her self-image, yet she told me her story as casually as if she were describing a shopping expedition. Again, this is a normal reaction in incest survivors, who have assimilated the "thorn in their paw" as if it is a normal part of life. They are, sadly, used to living with pain.

Guilt and Self-Blame

Deep down, Joanne believed that she contributed to the incest. "I could have stopped it if I wanted," was her recurring sentiment. "But I didn't stop it because part of me enjoyed it, so it must be my fault. I can't blame my uncle for what happened."

I've heard so many incest survivors echo Joanne's sentiments. They say, "It's my fault, because . . .

. . . I didn't say no."
. . . I acted seductively."
. . . I enjoyed it."
. . . I didn't tell anyone."
. . . we had a special relationship."

As adults, we must take responsibility for our own actions. But when we're children, are we responsible for our *inter*actions with adults? Isn't the adult the person truly responsible for the outcome of situations involving children? The adult, after all, is the one who controls the tempo, tone, and flavor of any situation. The adult has the power to coerce, force, and generally manipulate the child into doing whatever is intended. The adult can also create the illusion that the child is a willing partner.

For so many incest, molestation, and rape survivors, the basic human response to sexual arousal creates guilt and self-blame. From a physiological standpoint, if someone touches our genitals in a certain way, we become aroused. Our breathing becomes shallow and fast, our heart and pulse rates quicken, our vaginal walls thicken, and we excrete lubrication. We also feel pleasurable sensations in the clitoral region.

These feelings represent a physiological fact of life, yet sexual trauma survivors bear tremendous guilt as a result of these very human reactions. "I felt turned on" is the irrational logic, "so I must have contributed to the situation." The reality, of course, is that these victims were anything but consensual partners.

It may help to envision a pipeline running through your body, from the top of your head and out through your toes. This pipeline is what our normal human emotions run through. Normally, an emotion occurs, we feel energized by the feeling, and then the feeling dissipates and runs out the bottom of the pipeline.

Now, imagine that pipeline being clogged. Emotions become backed up, like clogged plumbing in a sink. Well, that's exactly what happens when guilt and self-blame occur—they act like blocks in our emotional pipeline, backing up strong feelings behind them.

The incest survivor blames herself. She also isolates herself—rarely if ever, revealing what transpired. If she does talk about it, she distances herself from the emotions connected to the incest, just as she did when the trauma originally occurred. During an incestuous encounter, children "shut off" their painful feelings of alarm and shame. Later, when they remember these incidents, these feelings usually remain detached from the person's true inner self.

The incest survivor usually feels "different" from other girls her age. She often feels damaged, as if something is terribly wrong with her. And she suspects that other people, even strangers, know that something's amiss. She expects to be rejected, disliked, and mistreated by others. She doesn't know the meaning of a trusting, intimate relationship where she can let her guard down.

So much isolation, so much self-loathing. The only way the incest survivor can concentrate on her adult responsibilities is to shut down all memories and emotions connected to the original pain. This is one of the primary reasons why she overeats. Food makes her feel numb and keeps the memories and emotions from surfacing. It also serves as a form of entertainment to counteract the boredom caused by her isolation, and gives her companionship and a feeling of "fullness" in contrast to the emptiness coursing through her soul.

If *you* are a person experiencing acute, stinging emotional pain, you are probably aware that food is a very quick fix. You're in so much pain that you quit caring whether you'll gain weight or not. You give up. You just want to feel better *now*, and you know exactly what will do it: food. Then, when the satisfying feelings of overeating wear off, you eat some more.

Food Helps You Forget

Food not only makes you feel calm and numb, it also quiets troublesome thoughts and memories. Take Cheryl's case, for example.

Cheryl's Story

Cheryl was depressed and having trouble losing weight when she checked into the women's psychiatric hospital where I was the Program Director. I worked closely with her to uncover her true issues.

A bright, highly educated woman, Cheryl's extra 50 pounds came from one primary source: the case of colas she consumed every day. She almost always had a can of cola in her hand, and she sipped it continually. What purpose was the cola serving? I wondered.

Since Cheryl had been through years of outpatient therapy, she was another "therapy-wise" client. She'd read dozens of self-help books and taken numerous psychology classes in college. She was also terrified of unearthing the pain she could feel just below the surface, deep inside of her. Cheryl's defenses were high, guarding against any undue anguish.

When Cheryl told me that she couldn't remember her

childhood before age 12, I knew, right away, that she was repressing some dreadful memories with her selective amnesia. Forgetting huge chunks of one's life is not something that people do on purpose; rather, it is a coping mechanism to avoid facing painful truths about their lives.

We decided that hypnosis would be an effective way to access Cheryl's hidden memories. During the first session, I asked Cheryl to describe the house she'd grown up in. She described it in brilliant detail, vividly giving me a "mental tour" of her house. Then, when I asked her to take me into her bedroom, she stopped. Another clue. She couldn't remember her bedroom.

The second session did yield a few details about her bedroom, though. She described waking up on a summer morning, with the light streaming in through her window. Now we had an "anchor," or a starting place, to initiate her memory retrieval, but she was still blocked.

I suspected that the colas were helping Cheryl silence her memories and feelings, so she agreed to abstain from all soda pop or other carbonated beverages. Since she was staying at the hospital, it was easier for her to adhere to this resolution.

Body Memories of Abuse

By our next session, Cheryl had been abstaining from colas for two days, and suddenly, the memories started flowing. Now, as I mentioned previously, there is a lot of controversy these days with respect to therapists "planting" ideas in clients' minds, especially where repressed memories of sexual abuse are concerned. I have seen overzealous, inexperienced counselors encourage clients to "recall" events that probably never happened. In fact, I've seen at least two clients diagnosed by other therapists as having a "multiple personality disorder" when it was unwarranted.

In Cheryl's case, her story was definitely her own. It was flowing from her without any prompting on my part. I played the part of a "blank slate therapist," one who neither exhibits pleasure nor disapproval while listening to what my client has to say. By doing so, the client is less apt to try to please the therapist by saying what she thinks the therapist wants to hear. Since compulsive overeaters are exquisitely sensitive to the reactions of other people (more than they are to their own), it's important for therapists to remain neutral with clients—warm, but neutral.

As Cheryl continued telling her story, she remembered her father coming into her bedroom while her mother was at work. Her father had been drinking, and he looked strange, with a faraway expression in his bloodshot eyes. He didn't waste any time: He pulled out his erect penis and forced Cheryl to take it in her mouth. He ejaculated almost immediately, and then left the bedroom, with Cheryl throwing up the semen onto her pillow.

She was terrified—too frightened to say anything to anyone about the horrendous act. As an only child without any other relatives, Cheryl didn't know whom to turn to. So she chose to forget. It never happened again, and her father never mentioned it. He died when Cheryl was 45, with the two never mentioning what had transpired that night. For all Cheryl knew, he was so drunk at the time that he may not have even remembered it himself.

I concluded that Cheryl's compulsion to drink soda was a reaction to the ejaculate in her mouth. As soon as we took the soda away, she began remembering. Her first clear memory was the sensation of her father's sharp pubic hairs pressed against her face. She kept saying, "It hurts, it hurts," during her early hypnosis sessions, so we made an effort to uncover the source of this "hurt." As soon as she remembered that it was her father's sharp pubic hair pressed hard against her face that caused the pain, she started to cry.

Cheryl allowed herself to recall the rest of the memories related to that incident over the next two sessions. We learned that the colas had kept the "body memories" of the incident—the sharp pubic hair, the smell of sweat and semen, and the taste and sensation of ejaculate—from resurfacing in Cheryl's mouth. The carbonation overrode the memories that she was cognizant of on a deeper level.

It's very common for the body to have haunting sensations, or "body memories," long after a trauma has occurred. Incest survivors who endure vaginal penetration often have gynecological disorders. I've worked with two survivors of forced anal sex who had colon problems. The body is crying out; it wants you to remember and release the pain.

When Cheryl finally did remember, and then released her pain in the ways described later on in this book, she didn't *need* colas anymore. Her subconscious need to "cleanse" her mouth with cola was obviated. And, since her caloric intake dropped dramatically, so too did her weight.

"I Don't Remember!"

What if—like Cheryl—you *suspect* that you've been sexually abused but you can't remember any specific incident? Well, there is no one right answer to that question. All I can do is present you with available options, and then you must choose which path is right for *you.*

There are many different schools of thought about repressed sexual abuse memories. Ellen Bass, co-author of the classic work on sexual abuse, *The Courage to Heal,* told me this: "If a woman thinks she's been sexually abused, then she has. Period." Bass says that no one thinks about sexual abuse, in the absence of real abuse occurring.

Other therapists scoff at this idea and actually go to the other extreme. One male psychiatrist told me that memories of sexual abuse are often "fantasies of women having sex with their fathers. It's a projection of their true wishes." Now, this theory—widely held by many Freudian psychiatrists—is dangerous as far as I'm concerned! I understand, and to some degree, accept, the Oedipus and Electra complex theories (that, as children, we coveted our parents as ideal love objects). But I don't think that our love for our fathers would lead to images of forced, painful sex! To imply this is to revictimize the victim and cause her further anguish. Sexual abuse survivors feel guilty enough without having a psychiatrist tell them that they made the whole thing up because they really wanted to sleep with their fathers!

To me, the truth lies somewhere between the psychiatric model and Bass's theory. During my work with abuse survivors, it struck me how everyone remembered their abuse *when they were ready.* I've worked with survivors in the 40- to 60-year-old range who have lived their whole lives—holding jobs and raising kids—without remembering their abuse.

Then, at some point in their lives, an amazing thing happened. The survivor had a glimmer of a memory, a fleeting picture of her father holding her down, or her brother's naked body. Some minuscule image, connected to powerful feelings of fear or rage, prompted the rest of the memories to pour out. She is haunted by disturbing memories and feelings of overwhelming grief for days, sometimes weeks, until she remembers everything.

It is clear that she was ready to remember.

I do believe that the quality of life improves dramatically once the memory is retrieved and the emotions have been worked through. Many middle-aged and elderly clients I've worked with have expressed remorse that they didn't get into therapy at an earlier age. They probably would have been lighter, happier, and freer throughout their lives had they worked on their sexual-abuse issues years before. Their overeating and weight gain would have presented less of a problem; in fact, these issues might not have been factors in their lives to begin with.

However, just as you can't unfurl the petals of a rose and make it bloom before it's ready, I don't think it's wise to force a survivor to remember before she's at the right place in her personal growth. She'll enter therapy when she's feeling a pain that is too great to handle alone.

Pain is a gift that forces us to do good things for ourselves— I truly believe that. Throughout her life, a woman who has endured an abusive situation often tends to focus on the needs of others. The only thing that makes her pay attention to herself is if her body SCREAMS at her through the conduit of emotional or physical pain. Her body and emotions demand that she listen.

In other words, the body is a perfectly engineered clock. Although selective amnesia is an incredible coping device, graciously allowing victims some semblance of sanity and peace of mind, the clock knows when it's time to remember. And it's a good thing it does, because a repressed memory is like a dormant volcano, with the lava of anger toward oneself and the perpetrator bubbling below the surface.

This below-the-surface activity creates a paradox. An island with a dormant volcano may appear to be a paradise, but that's an illusion because there's a continual buildup of tension as the inevitable explosion looms ahead. An abuse survivor with repressed memories is living with the same uneasiness—she may appear to have a happy, full life, but there is always something going on below the surface, something pervasive and menacing that leaves her soul hungry for freedom, happiness—and food.

Some Clues to Help You

If you suspect that you were sexually abused but are not quite sure, some detective work might be in order. Detectives, of course, use deductive reasoning to solve cases. Deductive reasoning means starting with a lot of clues and information and then narrowing the focus to only the most important facts. You can do the same thing.

To help you in your detective work, I have listed some traits, characteristics, and outcomes commonly exhibited by sexual abuse survivors. A word of caution, though: Many of these traits characterize other types of childhood trauma other than sexual abuse. So, use this list for general information only. If you already strongly suspect that you were sexually abused, then I would recommend exploring the issue further with a therapist trained in abuse counseling.

Traits and Characteristics Often Exhibited by
Sexual Abuse Survivors

Eating Disorders: Compulsive overeating, chronic dieting, yo-yo syndrome, anorexia, bulimia

Chemical Dependency: Alcohol abuse, drug addiction, prescription drug abuse

Sexual Difficulties: Promiscuity or avoidance of all sex, pain during intercourse, inability or extreme difficulty achieving orgasm

Sleep Disorders: Chronic nightmares, insomnia, oversleeping, lethargy

Lifestyle Issue: Inability to hold a job, chronic financial and legal problems, prostitution, irresponsibility, being disorganized or organized to a fault

Relationship Signals: Extreme rage toward one or more parents, inability to trust others, irrational fear of abandonment, insatiable need for reassurance, jealousy, suspicion, contempt for men

Body-Image Concerns: Compulsion to exercise and weigh oneself, avoidance of all exercise, obsession with plastic surgery, perfectionism with respect to dress and appearance

Social Issues: People-pleasing or complete isolation from others, being very guarded and protective, feeling a need to be in control of all situations, being compulsively late or punctual, self-centeredness or self-consciousness, grandiosity mixed with very low self-esteem, difficulty laughing or expressing any emotion, laughing too much as an obvious avoidance tactic

Health Signals: Chronic gynecological problems, colon or rectal disorders.

Most of these characteristics or traits involve normal behavior that is taken to the extreme, so again, it's important not to read too much into this list. It's not necessary to categorically label yourself as "a sexual abuse survivor" or not. What *is* of the utmost importance is to uncover and release the pain that is triggering your overeating.

Coming to Grips with the Unthinkable

— Another client, Delores, had abstained from her binge foods—high-fat cheeseburgers and french fries— for two weeks before her memories of incest came flooding to the surface. She was in a group therapy session at our outpatient clinic when she began crying, then screaming hysterically, all the while keeping her eyes tightly shut.

When she'd calmed a little bit, she told the group about the horrible image she'd just seen flashing through her mind: She remembered her father sodomizing her when she was a little girl. Although Delores knew that her sister had been molested by their father and had been in therapy for years, Delores thought that she'd come out untouched. What had actually happened, though, was that she'd blocked the memories of those few horrible times her father had raped her anally.

Delores had focused all her energies, instead, on helping her younger sister with her problems. She had always focused on other people, which was another way, besides overeating, to stifle her own thoughts. She joined our program because some of her co-workers were losing weight at our clinic. "If only I could lose 50 pounds, then I'd be happy," was her initial statement to the intake therapist. We never argued with clients who made statements such as this one, although we heard it all the time. We just let matters proceed along their course.

It's true that for some people, being overweight may be purely tied to genetics, a slow thyroid, or a sluggish metabolism. It just so happens that I've yet to meet anyone with those problems. Once they release the food (or beverages) that serve as a protective shield, just about every client I ever worked with has uncovered hidden memories or emotions that have eventually surfaced.

Sometimes the memories are already on the surface. My client, Terry, for instance, remembered every detail of the incestuous acts inflicted on her by her father and uncle. The trouble was, she remembered the incidents intellectually, without *feeling* any accompanying emotions. This is a phenomenon that I saw all the time, a very common scenario.

An incest survivor will often insist that "it was no big deal." She has a need to see herself as a survivor—which she certainly is. Because, in order to survive incest—an utter betrayal of trust on the part of a family member—one has to deal with one of the most excruciating traumas imaginable. But incest doesn't just make you stop trusting others; it makes you mistrust yourself.

You become guarded, defensive, isolated, and tough.

Talk-show host Oprah Winfrey has publicly discussed her own history of incest. Her uncle molested her in rural Tennessee, and although Oprah remembered and acknowledged the incest, it was in that emotionally devoid, intellectually based manner that I saw time and time again. And that's precisely why, after she lost all that weight on a liquid diet, she gained it back again.

She hadn't yet released her pain. But more on that topic later in this chapter. I want to get back to Terry.

Terry's Story

Terry grew up in the county next to where Oprah Winfrey was raised. She lived with her parents and an extended family out in the middle of nowhere, in a large farmhouse. There was no school in the vicinity, so Terry was schooled at home.

She recounted what happened to her when she was a little girl: "My uncle took me into his bedroom and said, 'Now it's time for you to become a lady.' Then he took off my clothes and underwear and he had sex with me. It hurt really, really bad. I was crying, but he wouldn't stop.

"Two days later, my father did the same thing. I had sex regularly with my uncle and my father. My mother and everyone else knew all about it, but everyone just accepted it. That's just the way things were done. My mother had sex with her father, and her mother had done the same before her. It's so sick, now that I know better, but it was a family custom."

Whenever Terry's father and uncle wanted sex, they'd tell Terry that it was their "special time," and she'd dutifully comply with the men. Years later, when Terry was enrolled in a public junior high school, she asked a classmate if she ever had "special times" with her father.

"Sure," the girl replied, "whenever my father and I go fishing together, that's a very special time."

Terry talked to the girl further and discovered that her definition of "special time" with her dad was quite different from the "special times" Terry was having with her father. Terry talked to another girl at school, and without revealing exactly why she was asking, Terry learned that her incestuous relationship was not normal at all.

Terry's only way out was to run away, and she became a street urchin of sorts, trying to survive by hustling and begging. She even sold her body for sex on a couple of occasions, just to get enough money to eat. By the time Terry checked into our psychiatric hospital, she had tried to commit suicide several times.

Terry was the ultimate "tough chick." Her short-cropped black hair and ultramasculine clothing, combined with her ever-present scowl, gave her a menacing presence. No one was going to get close to Terry. She pushed everyone away who tried to help her, screaming at the nurses and cussing at the counselors.

This behavior was a clue to what was actually going on inside, because often those who are the most unlovable are the ones who need the most love. Terry was definitely vying for the title, "Most Unlovable," and I knew that meant she needed extra love from others. The hospital staff ignored her rude comments and, instead, showered her with kind words and affection. We also asked her to put her thoughts down in a journal (we couldn't ask her to express feelings yet, as she wasn't in touch with them, and this request would have frustrated her).

Every night, Terry would pour her heart out into her journal. The next day, she would ask me to read her journal entries. I knew what she wanted: She was asking me to understand her. As much as Terry feared getting close to people, she also craved emotional intimacy. All people do. After all, connecting with others is a normal human need—that's why solitary confinement is the ultimate punishment in prison.

Here's one of Terry's journal entries that told me and the other staff members that Terry was getting in touch with her true self. Keep in mind that Terry was 37 years old at the time she wrote this:

I am a child. I know this because it is said that emotionally one stops growing up when child abuse starts. Well, that made sense to me. That gave me the answer to why I had a hard time coming across right with emotionally mature adults, and why I couldn't understand where the heck they were coming from.

My abuse started at the age of three or younger. I was drinking whiskey from a bottle, from what I had been told, when I was a little baby. So, how do I grow up? I wanted to just hurry and grow up! So . . . I worked hard in therapy, I read and studied recovery books, went to all the suggested meetings, and I put a lot of time every day into all these things so I could grow up real fast.

I couldn't understand it! I still threw fits of anger

when I felt rejected or hurt. I still felt empty inside, and I have been getting hugs from people, and people like me. I still hated myself when I knew that I really was okay. I couldn't get my head to catch up to my emotions.

But . . . I have grown up some now. I can see that I am defensive, and I can see that I am not coming across on the outside the way I really feel on the inside. Like, for example, when I don't like myself, I come across like the kid that says: No, I don't want anything. Go away. I don't always catch my attitude at the time, because I am into my own thoughts and feelings and not paying attention to how my actions are being perceived. And that makes me feel worse, so I hurt myself, isolate, and am harder on myself still.

I know that part of growing up is learning how to take responsibility for my own actions. Heck, I would hit myself, starve myself, binge on food until my stomach hurt, send people away from me, and even just go try and die so I wouldn't feel so bad about messing up!

Terry was clearly craving human interaction. At the same time, she saw herself as being very different—even less than—other people. She wanted to be accepted, but was terrified of being rejected or abandoned, so the bottom line was that she couldn't bear to be hurt again so she avoided any situation that was potentially painful. As difficult as loneliness is, it hurts less than being rejected. So, instead of risking rejection, Terry rejected others first.

As insensitive as Terry seemed to the outside world, she was exquisitely sensitive on the inside. In another journal entry, Terry chronicled her struggle with her vulnerability issues:

I do not want to admit that I am in need of support, that I can't handle things all on my own, the way I think I should be able to handle them. So . . . I don't tell anyone.

I have even found myself griping about things that don't even matter, coming across in a hateful way even with nitpicky things, trying to detach from the love and the caring that I have for the hospital staff. Even when I get a hug from you, I then run away. And I am still having a hard time letting you all know my needs, so I just let you all think that I don't need anything, even when you ask me, and I end up in crisis from not getting those needs met. Then I tell you when it's almost too late.

When I am mad at myself, I definitely don't want any of you around me, because you don't deserve to be around someone as bad as me, and I may even have the face of anger, but it's not toward any of you. It is toward me.

Trusting Others, Trusting Self

Terry, like other sexual abuse survivors, was struggling with trust issues. We human beings learn how to trust others from the moment we're born. Normally, a baby cries, and her mother or father takes care of her needs. She learns that the world responds to her and takes care of her.

A baby or child who is sexually violated feels physical pain—it *hurts* to have foreign objects inserted into your vaginal or rectal region. So, she cries. But the pain doesn't stop—instead, it gets worse.

If a parent is the sexual abuser, the child still feels that her trust was violated. I've worked with people who were sexually abused by adult authority figures such as doctors, teachers, priests and baby-sitters, and they were shattered by the experience. Usually, trust is then replaced with fear. This person trusted an adult to treat her nicely, and that trust was betrayed. In addition, she instinctively wonders why Mommy and Daddy didn't protect her from the abuser.

There's Not Enough Chocolate in the World . . .

Most of the early childhood sexual abuse survivors I've worked with described feeling something akin to a "big empty hole" in the center of their being. They felt empty and incomplete, and there was an urge to relieve the feeling of emptiness, as well as the self-doubt, fear, and anger that resided there. The best way they could think of to fill that hole was by eating a lot of fattening, starchy foods. And, in some cases, other compulsive behavior, such as shopping, drinking, or addictive relationships took the place of compulsive overeating.

But nothing—nothing—ever completely fills the chasm. There just isn't enough chocolate cake in the world to quiet the pangs of emptiness. No matter how much she eats, the abuse survivor just can't escape the echoes emanating from the hollow drum in her middle.

I've always remembered the line from the play *Les Miserables*: "There's a grief that can't be spoken. There's a pain, goes on and on." Well, for abuse survivors, the emotional pain they feel is beyond words. It's a chronic, intense gnawing that they've almost gotten used to as a result of living with it for so long. But, a basic instinct of living creatures is to extinguish pain when one feels it. An animal whose foot is caught in a trap will chew off his limb to escape. Abuse survivors who compulsively overeat are doing the same thing.

When your overeating stems from emotional need, there's an urgency attached to this behavior. And a seemingly endless amount of emptiness and hunger. No matter how much you eat, you never feel full or satisfied. You want more food, more sedation, more comfort, more love.

Food temporarily eases the hollow feeling within you, but not for long. It's as if food is hypnotizing you, and as soon as the hypnotic trance is broken, you need more food to remain in a state of not-so-blissful ignorance.

But there *is* a way out of this maze. I promise you.

chapter eight

ADOLESCENT AND
ADULTHOOD SEXUAL TRAUMAS

*"Nothing in life is to be feared.
It is only to be understood."*
— Madame Curie

While a child is especially vulnerable to abuse due to her small stature and trusting, innocent nature, adolescents and adults are also ripe for psychological and physical abuse.

Dating and/or marrying the wrong man is one of the primary factors leading to an abusive situation in a woman's life—my own included. Many women will become involved with a man who, at first glance, seems to be the epitome of Prince Charming. Only later do we discover his dark, stormy side. A woman who was fortunate enough to be raised in a loving, supportive family devoid of abuse will recognize the man as someone who is sick and in need of professional help. Such a woman will then take one of two avenues: She will either insist that the sick man receive help of some kind, or she will leave him. Only a woman who grew up thinking that abuse is normal would try to change, or stay in a relationship with a morose or volatile man.

Yet, many women do stick with abusive boyfriends and husbands through hell and high water—mostly through hell. And while I only advocate divorce as a last-ditch measure, many of my clients found that that was the only way to end their pain. Of course, divorce and romantic breakups bring on a new set of problems altogether, which is why many women continue to overeat even after leaving abusive men. If you were born into pain, you carry it within your own self. Divorce doesn't automatically create rainbows in the sky and birds merrily chirping in the trees. However, I have certainly witnessed a lot of positive changes occurring in women who extricated themselves from bad marriages.

"You Would If You Loved Me": Abusive Boyfriends

— Melody, a 19-year-old stunning blue-eyed blonde, sat in my office crying uncontrollably. Her boyfriend, Mark, had just dropped her off for her therapy session and they'd had an intense argument on the way over.

"He called me a . . . a"—she could barely say the words— ". . . a fucking bitch!" Melody cried, her face contorted with shock and rage. "Nobody has ever, ever called me that before!" She continued blowing her nose and rocking herself in my office chair.

Why do young women like Melody, the picture of beauty and promise, become attracted to, and then remain with, abusive boyfriends such as Mark? Unfortunately, the majority of teen clients I've worked with are just like Melody—crushed by low self-esteem, and counting on a "cool" boyfriend to provide love, companionship, and social status. What they usually don't count on is the hot temper and insensitive nature often common to these "cool guys."

Mark, like many of my clients' boyfriends, smoked marijuana and drank beer daily. Naturally, he downplayed the impact that these substances had on his psyche: "It's just pot and beer. At least it ain't crack cocaine and hard liquor!"

But marijuana, as I've found through working with people with addictive personalities, is often the cause of erratic mood swings. After lighting up a joint, the pot smoker can be calm and euphoric and pleasant to be around; or he can be silly, immature, and obnoxious. After he comes down, he is often extremely grouchy and irritable. As a result, his girlfriend has to walk on eggshells around him to avoid triggering a verbal tirade or physical battery.

However, the pot smoker will swear that this isn't so. "Just give me another joint and I'll be normal again," he'll say. Then we therapists are left to pick up the pieces when their girlfriends are victimized by psychological or physical abuse once again.

So, I reiterate: Why would a girl or woman want to associate with a guy who treats her with a lack of respect? The answer, of course, is that she has either grown up believing that this sort of abuse is normal, or because she doesn't believe she deserves—or can find—anyone better. Furthermore, she probably blames herself for the man's harsh words and actions.

The sentiment is always: *If only I could* ["lose weight," "look sexier," "act sweeter," "give him oral sex," etc.], *then he'll treat me better.* She desperately wants to be able to predict and control his outbursts of temper. Occasionally, when she finds something that seems to work ("I fixed him his favorite dinner, and he calmed down"), she'll become unrealistically attached to that behavior. Unfortunately, the man soon finds something else to be upset about, and she has to start all over again, looking for the magic formula to mitigate his unpredictable moods.

My work with young women such as Melody involves buoying up their self-esteem (almost to the extreme). And while I couldn't tell Melody to leave Mark, I did urge her to protect herself against an unwanted pregnancy and sexually transmitted diseases. It's heartbreaking to see a woman in a shaky relationship get pregnant and then decide she has no choice but to marry the baby's father. That situation points to eventual divorce, and by that time, she may have borne additional children whom she will have to support.

What follows are some poignant cases of young women I worked with who carried pounds of pain triggered by boyfriend abuse:

— Yolanda complained that Bob, her new boyfriend, "was never around." When I asked her to expand on this statement, it turned out that Bob was actually dating—and sleeping with—two other young women. "He says he loves all of us," Yolanda told me, "but he can't decide who he should marry, so he needs to date all of us. He needs to . . . go to bed with all of us, and then he'll decide which one of us to pick."

The insecurities that Yolanda had developed while waiting to be "chosen" as the winner of this sick beauty pageant had driven her to snack incessantly on fattening foods such as chips, pretzels, and nuts. She'd actually gained ten pounds within a month, a fact that did not go unnoticed by Bob. "He complained that my butt's getting too big," Yolanda blurted out with a pained expression on her face. "I know if I get fat, Bob won't pick me, but I can't stop eating!"

— Lucinda's live-in boyfriend of three years, Jim, had recently hit her across the face. She now sported a big black eye, which she was unsuccessfully trying to mask with makeup. Unbelievably, Lucinda blamed herself: "He's pissed off at me 'cause I can't find a job. He says he's sick of carrying all the weight, so he wanted to get it through to me how much pressure he's under. I know he never would have hit me if I had a job."

To calm Jim's fiery temper, Lucinda would prepare elaborate meals and desserts. The only problem was, Lucinda would end up consuming most of the food. It turned out that she was compulsively overeating to quell her tension and anxiety over her job situation.

— Sixteen-year-old Lisa's boyfriend, Frank, never hit her—at least not with his fists. Frank's weapon of choice was words. A very controlling and jealous young man, Frank was constantly accusing Lisa of cheating on him. If Lisa visited a girlfriend, Frank would call two or three times to see if Lisa was really there. Afterward, he would grill her about the possible presence of other guys at her friend's house.

As a result, Lisa lived in perpetual fear that she'd trigger a jealous rage in Frank. Lisa, like so many women, was taking responsibility for Frank's behavior and bad moods. When I asked her what she was getting out of this relationship, Lisa would explain that Frank's jealousy just proved how much he loved her.

Lisa's weight was a direct result of the turmoil in her relationship. She was determined to lose 15 pounds, but as soon as her weight started dropping and her figure began to shape up, Frank would go crazy with suspicion and jealousy. "He's sure I'm trying to lose weight to attract another boyfriend," Lisa complained.

— Connie's boyfriend, Tim, was committing the ultimate abusive and manipulative act: He was constantly threatening to commit suicide if she ever left him. Any woman who has been on the receiving end of this type of emotional blackmail experiences enormous feelings of responsibility and guilt. She feels trapped in the relationship, fearing that her boyfriend will kill himself if she leaves, and that she'd never be able to forgive herself if that happened.

One night after Connie tried to break up with Tim, he locked himself in his car and put a gun to his head while Connie stood by helplessly. "I'm gonna do it! I'm gonna shoot myself!" Tim kept taunting. "It'll be all your fault, too!" Connie was beside herself with panic and horror. The weight of this pressure led her to binge on high-fat foods. Somehow, when Connie was eating a cheeseburger, she didn't feel quite so bad about Tim. After she'd gained 20 pounds, she decided to stay with Tim, rationalizing that she was lucky that he didn't criticize her for being overweight.

Date and Acquaintance Rape

Most women discover early on that young men are unusually interested in sex. In most cases, she first discovers this truth when a date is coming to an end and her companion sticks his hand under her blouse. At that point, she must grapple with the questions all women face while growing up: How far do I let him go? If I give in, will he lose all respect for me? If I don't give him what he wants, will he dump me for some girl who will?

For the guy, the question is usually answered without much hesitation: Yes, I want sex—now! For the girl, the dilemma is much more complicated and can result in serious consequences. *She's* the one who would get a bad reputation. *She's* the one who would get pregnant. *She's* the one who stands to lose him if she says no.

Sandra's Story

Sixteen-year-old Sandra was on her first date with Matt, a popular quarterback on the high school football team. On the way home from the movie they'd just seen, Matt drove his car to a secluded spot and the two of them made out passionately. Sandra, a virgin, enjoyed Matt's kisses and the feel of his muscular arms around her body. But when he reached up under her skirt, Sandra protested.

"Come on, Sandra," he said in response to her resistance, "I want you so much. Don't be a tease." Sandra pushed his hand off her legs, but Matt's grip got stronger and more forceful. Sandra tried with all her might to pull away, but she was no match for the determined athlete. He pushed her skirt up and, while pinning her down with his body, Matt forcibly stuck his fingers in her vagina.

"Ouch!" Sandra started yelling at the top of her lungs. "Stop! You're hurting me!"

Since he couldn't stifle her screams, Matt angrily lifted himself off of Sandra's squirming body. "Get out!"

he ordered. Then he drove off with tires squealing, leaving Sandra to walk the two miles back home in the dark.

The next morning at school, several kids looked at Sandra with funny expressions. In fact, she noticed that people were treating her different all day, some giggling as she walked by, others avoiding making eye contact with her.

Matt hadn't wasted any time. He had starting spreading ugly rumors—saying that he'd "done Sandra" the night before. He embellished the story further, making her sound "easy" and promiscuous. Now her peers were ostracizing her.

During the months that followed, Sandra become increasingly isolated from her classmates. She walked home alone, and she never left the house on weekends. Instead, she turned to food for comfort and companionship—and gained 15 pounds by the end of her junior year.

Date rape (or attempted date rape) is a common occurrence among adult women as well. Take my client Janice's case, for example.

— Janice's date, Gus, had nonconsensual sex with her after she passed out from a night of drinking too much wine. She blamed herself for drinking too much, but that didn't keep her from manifesting symptoms of "Rape Syndrome."

She became depressed and started overeating and oversleeping. She isolated herself from her friends, and neglected her normal grooming and housecleaning habits. Janice became so suspicious of the men that she'd meet that she wouldn't accept any dates—even when that nice co-worker of hers that she'd been dying to meet asked her out.

As is the case with date-rape survivors such as those mentioned above, acquaintance-rape victims comprise another segment of the female population that often indulges in self-blame for an act that was perpetrated upon them without their volition. These women tend to turn their anger away from the perpetrator and toward themselves, most often resulting in depression and a marked lack of self-esteem.

— Lynne was moving out of her apartment when the man who lived across the hall asked if she needed help. She gratefully accepted his offer, saying that she could use some assistance carting the big box of dishes down to her car. The man entered the apartment, closed the door, and then forcibly raped her.

Lynne never called the police, figuring they'd blame her for having the "stupidity to invite a near-stranger into my apartment." She suffered tremendous guilt and mentally berated herself for being "so stupid." Two months later, she quit her job and returned to her hometown to live with her parents.

Feeling like a helpless, incompetent little girl, Lynne readily returned to her girlhood eating habits. She binged on her mother's home-cooked meals and desserts and abandoned the exercise regimen she had established over the years. By the time she came in for therapy, Lynne was convinced that she had lost the capacity to achieve anything of value in life.

The Ultimate Violation—Rape by a Stranger

When a woman is forced to submit to sexual intercourse, it is "rape." Usually, this act of violence occurs without warning, and the victim is not only hurt physically, but is terrorized psychologically as well. The rapist's sick fantasy often involves punishing a woman for the perceived crimes of other females he's been involved with—his mother, ex-wife, or girlfriend. He may have reached the point where his only means of pleasure or sexual satisfaction is through humiliating and controlling his female victim. Bottom line: The rape has little to do with sex, and everything to do with power.

In addition to the vicious act of rape itself, the perpetrator may verbally assault his victim, force her to engage in revolting acts such as eating excrement, and make her believe that he'll kill her if she doesn't submit to him. So, in the midst of one of the most degrading and nightmarish experiences of this woman's life, she is also coping with the fear of death.

Rapists often use weapons such as knives or hammers, which leave permanent scars on their victims. One woman I worked with had her skull bashed in and had to undergo many reconstructive surgeries. Another woman had her hair hacked off during a gang rape.

The victim is humiliated. She is horrified. She wants to disappear.

The post-traumatic shock disorder accompanying the act of rape leaves a variety of symptoms in its wake, including:

- Sleep disorders: insomnia, oversleeping, night terrors and sweats, repeated nightmares about the attack

- Feelings of jumpiness and insecurity; agoraphobia

- Abuse of alcohol, drugs, or food

- Sexual disorders, encompassing both a lack of desire for sex or extreme promiscuity

- Relationship difficulties: feeling irritable, argumentative, defensive, secretive, and exhibiting wide mood swings

- Involuntarily reliving the experience

In light of the many problems that must be dealt with, most rape survivors derive beneficial results from treatment with a knowledgeable therapist, who will point out that a great deal that they're experiencing is tied in to two issues:

1. Feeling a lack of control over their personal safety.

2. Blaming themselves. This is really an attempt to regain a feeling of control. "If only I hadn't walked down that street," etc., is a way for the victim to reassure herself that if she takes the proper precautions from now on, she will be safe.

One study conducted a few years back (Bownes, I. T. et al. 1990) found that in a sample of 51 rape survivors, 70 percent exhibited symptoms of post-traumatic stress disorder, which made them especially prone to anxiety and depression.

Some of the rape survivors I've worked with were also guilt-ridden with respect to the response they had to penile penetration—that is, vaginal lubrication. Incest and rape survivors alike secretly chastise themselves for this normal physiological reaction. What they learn in therapy is that, just because the body may have responded to the rape or incest with certain feelings (some involving pleasure) it doesn't mean that they themselves actually enjoyed the act. The vaginal lubrication itself is in response to any stimulation—an involuntary reflex that is out of the victim's control. So, she learns to focus on the more crucial issues: the physical pain involved, the violation of her rights, the nonconsensual sex, and so on. She didn't ask for, or do anything to cause, the act of rape or incest, and she needs to stop blaming herself.

The shame she feels is one of the FATS feelings—Fear, Anger, Tension, and Shame—that triggers the desire to overeat. As you read further, your healing will continue to unfold, so it's important to note that a primary ingredient in the healing process is turning shame and accompanying self-blame into forgiveness. As soon as you transform Fear, Anger, Tension, and Shame into Forgiving, Accepting, and Trusting your Self, you can make the final leap to Forget All That Stuff—and put the pain and the pounds behind you.

PART II

Releasing Your Pounds of Pain

chapter nine

REMEMBERING AND
RELEASING THE PAIN

*"Courage is resistance to fear, mastery
of fear—not absence of fear."*
— Mark Twain

You've now read about many different types of people who have put on pounds of pain as a result of various traumatic situations. Maybe you've only seen yourself portrayed in several of the case studies; perhaps only one or two struck a chord. I've offered a degree of therapeutic guidance throughout this book so far, but it probably still feels as if the pain and excess pounds are here to stay.

In this chapter, and those that follow, I'll help you do the groundwork necessary to completely release your pain so you won't feel a need to hold on to your extra pounds.

Whose Fault Is It Anyway?

Children who experience emotional pain blame themselves. They're too young to understand when someone else—especially an adult—commits a wrongful act, it is *that* person's fault and not their own. The closest that children come to blaming others is when they point the finger at a brother, sister, or peer. Children rarely, if ever, point the finger at Mom, Dad, or other adults.

Instead, the child is conditioned to think along these lines: "If Daddy is being this mean to me, then he must be very, very angry. I must be a very bad girl to make Daddy this mad." If an abusive situation continues, the child's negative thinking progresses to an even greater extent: "If it's my fault that this horrible thing is happening, then I must be a horrible person."

As small children, we're not responsible for the bad things that happen to us. We're naturally irresponsible beings who don't know any better. We learn responsibility in three ways: (1) by heeding the lessons taught us by our parents and other authority figures; (2) by modeling the responsible behavior we see in our parents and others; and (3) by learning the hard way through trial and error. All these methods take time; we don't actually have a firm grasp on the "rules" until we're older.

However, as soon as we do begin to differentiate between right and wrong, we (if we're basically well-behaved kids) follow our parents' rules because it feels so good to get their approval, and it feels so bad to incur their disapproval. We still don't completely understand the rationale behind these rules; we only understand the consequences of not following them.

The onset of mature thinking is evinced when the older child or adolescent starts to "take the role of the other." This means that the child is able to view the world through the other person's eyes. The child can imagine how someone else feels and thinks—that is, she empathizes. At this stage, the child begins to understand that Mommy and Daddy aren't superhuman—they're simply people who experience joy, pain, confusion, and stress, just like anyone else. At this point in the child's development, she sees that the parent is capable of making a mistake or acting out of poor judgment.

It's also at this stage that many abuse survivors begin feeling sorry for their abusers. That's especially tragic, because it's absolutely necessary for the abuse survivor to acknowledge one very important point when healing herself from abuse: The adult was *entirely* responsible for the abusive act. And along with that acknowledgment and understanding comes the accompanying anger toward the perpetrator, as well as toward the act itself.

Repressed Pain, Forgotten Memories

By the time an abused child is age six or seven, she may have experienced so much emotional neglect or psychological, physical, or sexual battery that she doesn't know any other way of life. Pain is normal to her. She may have even repressed (forgotten) the abuse. And while an abused adult has access to support groups, reading materials, and health professionals, a child in this situation has few resources to help her deal with the trauma. She must rely on her wits, imagination, and sheer intestinal fortitude to endure the pain. Many abuse survivors I've worked with have actually learned to split their awareness in two during an abusive incident.

— My client Rebecca, for example, remembers being beaten by her parents. She would curl herself up into a fetal position and try to will herself to disappear during the beatings. Sometimes she imagined that she was leaving her body and that her soul was up on the ceiling, watching her father whipping her body. That was her way of dealing with incomprehensible pain.

Many children enter into this form of splitting off from reality, or *dissociation.* The word literally means "dis-associating yourself" from the situation. For children, dissociating may be their only escape route from abuse, and it often evolves into a routine coping mechanism as the child gets older.

Sometimes, painful childhood memories are repressed so deeply that the adult survivor honestly doesn't remember any of the abuse. At least, she doesn't *consciously* remember. Now, this would be an acceptable state of affairs if the underlying symptoms of abuse weren't so disruptive. If the abuse survivor grew up with a healthy body and mind, enjoying full and satisfying interpersonal relationships, then I'd be the first person to say that it's just as well she doesn't remember the horror she's gone through. Why dwell on such pain unless it serves some useful purpose?

Unfortunately, most survivors—whether they've forgotten the abuse or not—have a lava pit of anger bubbling deep within them. This anger manifests itself in chronic health problems such as cancer, gynecological disorders, back or neck pain, migraines, hemorrhoids, heart palpitations, skin problems, insomnia, alcoholism, and obesity. The abuse survivor usually doesn't have a very happy adult life. She probably has difficulties maintaining relationships, and she may hate her job.

But worst of all, she may hate herself. As an outgrowth of this self-loathing, she ends up neglecting her physical health. She overeats and avoids exercise because she doesn't believe that she deserves to have an attractive body. Other people are worthy of beauty; other people deserve good. Not me. I'm bad.

That is why she *must* remember the abuse. She must remember so she can tell her inner child—the little girl living inside her—that she isn't to blame for the bad things that happened. She must hug that little girl and explain that the perpetrator was the one responsible for the abuse.

This news will make the little girl angry. Very, very angry. After all, it's an injustice to harm a little child! How dare he hurt her!

It's when she has finally come to this realization that the anger—and most of the pain—will be released.

False Memories?

As I've discussed previously, a lot of the afternoon talk shows have featured "therapists" who say that it's not possible to completely repress memories of abuse. Well, I know, from my dealings with thousands of abuse survivors, that repression *is* an extremely common coping mechanism.

However, many women don't remember the abuse they experienced until a dramatic life event occurs. My client Tracy had completely pushed the memory of incest out of her conscious awareness. If you'd asked her, she'd swear that she had a perfect home life, with perfect parents. As I stated before, though, people who insist that everything was "perfect" while growing up are often abuse survivors who are overcompensating in order to keep a tight lid on an unexamined and painful childhood. It's a "No, I won't look at it! I can't bear to look!" syndrome.

Tracy's memories of being molested and being the victim of forced oral sex didn't surface until she'd given birth to a little girl of her own—a phenomenon that is very common. A woman often doesn't recall her own girlhood trauma until she has a baby girl. She tends to "see" herself in this little girl, and then usually remembers the traumatic incident.

It's true that an inexperienced or overly zealous therapist can convince someone she was abused, even if she wasn't. I've seen this happen, and the results can rip apart. But even in these "false memory" cases, there's something's going on there with the patient who has the false memory. She must have experienced some sort of emotional distress or parental neglect, or a therapist wouldn't be able to wield such power over her in the first place. Somewhere in her past, she learned to relinquish control.

Now, why would people want to identify themselves as an abuse survivors unless something had actually happened? Well, if they need an "identity" that much, then something is sorely missing from their lives.

It's a little like the case of some men I saw in psychotherapy many years ago who were posing as Vietnam vets suffering from post-traumatic stress disorder. These men had never served in Vietnam, yet they recounted graphically detailed war stories for me and the rest of the psychiatric hospital staff. One man burst into tears as he described his buddy's body being blown up in front of him. Later, when the staff discovered that these men were posing as vets, we were all understandably upset and confused.

However, we all knew one thing for certain: Even if these men didn't suffer from post-traumatic stress disorder from the war, they were definitely sick and in need of help. Why else would they embrace such a dramatic identity? Why did they need so much attention—psychiatric attention at that?

Well, I believe "false memory incest survivors" are in similar straits. They may not have actually experienced incest, but there's definitely something wrong—some pain somewhere is triggering their cry for help. I think that instead of criticizing and dismissing them, we need to focus on helping them.

Most Don't Forget

Most abuse survivors don't repress or forget their painful pasts. Instead, they minimize what happened. In essence, they shrug their shoulders and say, "Yes, this happened, but so what? It's over, and there's nothing I can do to change that now."

True. The past is the past. But if you're chronically overeating, that's a clear signal that the past is haunting you now. So let's take care of the problem right now. You could wait for a better, less hectic time in your life in order to confront the ghosts of your past, but that time will never arrive, will it? There will never be complete tranquility in your life—not until you address these issues, anyway.

Many abuse survivors minimize their painful pasts by downplaying how bad it was. "Yes, my brother molested me, but I'm strong so it didn't bother me as much as it could have," or "It's true that he forced me to have sex, but I can deal with it okay," or "It wasn't that bad, so I don't want to dwell on it."

This type of minimization is just one more defense mechanism shielding the survivor from pain. If you decide that "it's not that bad," then you won't feel as if you'll explode from the rage. You won't "go crazy," wondering, *Why me? Why me?*

Also, if you've lived with this memory for 10, 20, 30 years or more, it becomes old news in your mind. You've lived with the pain so long, it seems to be a part of you. *But just because you're used to it, it doesn't mean it hasn't affected you.* Those are two separate issues.

I'm asking you now to briefly reexperience the pain you endured as a child. I know that if you do, you'll walk through a "wall" within yourself. And beyond that wall lies greater peace of mind, the ability to love and relax, and a reduction in your appetite for food. Please trust that my years of working with abuse survivors has taught me that if you allow yourself to face this pain, you will lift the veil that is darkening your spirits.

You see, your natural, normal state is one that experiences happiness and contentment. God created you so you could enjoy life and feel pleasure. He wants you to feel joyous and free as you go about your daily activities—not bogged down with guilt and frustration.

Your true self is light in body and spirit. Why not release it by summoning up the courage to slay the dragons of your past. What have you got to lose but the misery . . . and the pounds?

chapter ten

THE TRUE YOU IS LIGHT
IN BODY AND SPIRIT

*"Faith therefore is to believe that which you do not see,
truth is to see what you have believed."*
— St. Augustine

Your true being, the way God created you, is someone who feels safe, secure, and happy. The true inner you is a free-spirited and loving little girl who embraces life and rejoices in its pleasures. She is thoughtful and giving, both to others and herself. She balances duty and play and doesn't feel guilty about relaxing and recharging her batteries.

As we've seen, the essence of this true being gets distorted by childhood pain and abuse. The immature child blames herself for this abuse and turns the anger—which rightfully belongs to the abuser—on herself. She eats to cover up the pain, as well as to punish herself for being "unworthy and bad." But the true being is still there, deep inside. She never leaves, because she was originally created mentally and physically healthy. She has simply become distorted, like a child seeing herself in a fun-house mirror.

Four primary emotions are products of this distortion, ones that trigger overeating episodes in female abuse survivors. They are Fear, Anger, Tension, and Shame—our FATS feelings . . . that make us fat!

However, it always seems that we're more aware of the hunger for food than we are of the emotions that precipitate it. It's very common for abuse survivors to be out of touch with their feelings, opinions, and bodily sensations.

— For example, my client Monica swore that she was never angry even though she was always clenching her jaw and fists. Another client, Suzanne, had adapted to her explosively abusive household by being super-agreeable to everyone. She had no idea what her own opinions were on politics, abortion, religion, or anything that mattered (even whether she enjoyed a movie or not); she was too afraid of offending someone and risking an outburst of anger. Still another client, Rosie, was not aware that her too-tight shoes, clothing, and bra were pinching and hurting her. She had learned—from years of abuse—how to turn off her awareness of pain and discomfort.

These clients, and others I've worked with, were frustrated by psychologists and self-help books that implored them to "get in touch with their feelings." Monica, Suzanne, Rosie, and other abuse survivors had no idea what a "feeling" was in the first place! While they may have felt some degree of empathy, guilt, frustration, subdued anger, and tepid romantic love, for the most part their access to the normal wide range of human emotions has been distorted and blunted.

I've found that the best way to begin working with an abuse

survivor is to ask her to start with the basics. So, if you've been a victim of abuse, I'm going to ask you at this very moment to become aware of the sensation of your body sitting on your chair. Notice how your back feels against the chair, and how your bottom feels. Does the chair feel hard or cushiony? Warm or cool? Is the fabric scratchy or soft?

How about your feet? Are they relaxed? Are your shoes tight and stiff, or flexible and light? Are your feet too cold, warm, or just right?

What about your clothing? Is your bra confining you in any way? How about your underwear, including pantyhose or stockings? Is the waistband of your pants, skirt, or dress comfortable? Does it bind you at all, or is it okay just as it is?

Where are your hands right now? Does their position signal relaxation or tension? How about your jaw—is it tight or sore in any way? Or is it relaxed?

Becoming aware of the sensations in each part of your body is an important first step in recognizing and acknowledging the other parts of your true being.

Recognizing Your FATS Signals

What's the difference between normal physical hunger and the hunger brought on by Fear, Anger, Tension, and Shame? Since it takes time to learn how to recognize FATS feelings, here's a good clue: Physical hunger is gradual, while emotional hunger happens instantly.

With physical hunger, your body will give you slowly evolving signals that your body wants to eat. First, you'll feel a little gnawing in your stomach. Then, you'll notice a slight hunger pang and your stomach may growl with emptiness. Eventually, you'll be driven to eat out of necessity.

With emotional hunger—triggered by the FATS feelings—your hunger suddenly speeds up from 0 to 100 miles an hour. One minute, you're not even thinking about food. The next, you're starving! This isn't physical hunger; it's definitely emotional.

Emotions are relayed to awareness in much the same way that radio signals are. If we have our "radio"—that is, our awareness of our emotions—tuned in to the right frequency, we'll know exactly what we're feeling most of the time. Many abuse survivors learn at a very young age that survival depends on tuning in their "radios" to the adult abusers around them. They become exquisitely sensitive to everyone around them, as Dianne was:

— Dianne never knew when her alcoholic father's temper would explode, so she learned to be tuned in to his moods. In this way, she could feel some semblance of control in an otherwise chaotic situation. Dianne tuned out her own feelings of fear, and tuned in her father's "frequency" so she could anticipate his behavior. This was the system she used in order to avoid beatings.

As an adult, Dianne's radio was still tuned off to her own frequency. She was one of the sweetest people you'd ever want to meet, but at 225 pounds, she wasn't really very happy with herself. Dianne's early childhood survival mechanism turned her into a major people-pleaser, afraid of listening to her own feelings.

The first fattening feeling Dianne and I worked on in therapy was . . .

Fear

Overeating in response to fear is very normal, due to the calming effects of food. Overeating episodes are triggered by many different manifestations of fear:

- *Insecurity.* Feeling like you're unqualified, don't deserve good things, or that you don't fit in; feeling fat in clothing; feeling like an "imposter" or a fake; feeling unprepared for an important event such as a presentation, speech, test, or job interview.

- *Walking on eggshells.* Fear that your ill-tempered spouse, boss, parent, or whoever will explode if you say or do something wrong; fear that you'll lose your job for the slightest dereliction of duty.

- *Generalized fear.* A feeling of impending doom; fear that if something good happens, then bad is sure to follow (as if there's a cause-and-effect relationship); overwhelming and unrealistic fears of trauma (such as being murdered, burning in a fire, being killed in an accident); jittery nervousness triggered by post-traumatic stress.

- *Abandonment fears.* Constant fear that your lover or spouse will leave you or cheat on you; fear that your friends don't like you; fear that your parents will die; fear of being alone.

- *Existential fears.* Fear that your life has no meaning or purpose; fear that you're "missing the boat" or missing out on wonderful opportunities; fear that you're a "nothing," or a hollow being.

- *Control issues.* Fear that others are trying to control you; fear of authority figures; fear of taking responsibility for yourself; phobias connected to driving a car or being in an airplane; fear of being vulnerable and getting hurt; fear of commitment and/or marriage.

- *Sexual fears.* Fear of the opposite sex in general; fear of receiving attention from, or talking to, the opposite sex; fear of sexual relations; fear of attracting sexual attention.

- *Intimacy Fears.* Fear of showing your true colors (others might reject the "real" you); fear of getting close to someone (they might abandon you).

Later on, you'll read about the methods my clients use to overcome Fear and the other FATS feelings. For now, let's continue learning how to recognize the emotions that trigger an excessive appetite for food.

Anger

There's nothing inherently wrong with anger. Yet it is the number-one emotion triggering compulsive overeating, especially in women. Much of our training as young girls teaches us to minimize, downplay, and disguise our feelings of anger—after all, it's not "ladylike" to scream and yell, is it?

Anger is a normal emotion in response to a perceived wrong. We're angry when we're born, due to the trauma of birth. We're angry as babies when we feel hungry, thirsty, wet, or tired. As children, we get angry at classmates who hit us, or little brothers who steal our toys.

However, as adolescents, the social pressure to "act like a lady" starts taking hold, and we begin to turn the anger inward. Instead of being angry at the stupid system of choosing kids for school sports teams during gym class, we feel sad when we're chosen last. We feel ugly when our first boyfriend breaks up with us. We feel humiliated when the popular kids poke fun at us. We blame ourselves for wrongs and feel depressed, instead of expressing anger outwardly. Is it any wonder that in adolescence, girls' self-esteem drops way below the level of boys'?

Abuse survivors blame themselves for the incest and molestation that occurred in the past, and rape survivors blame themselves as well. However, when we reach adulthood, anger is often no easier to deal with or admit to than when we were children. Take Martha, for example.

— Martha worked as a customer service representative for a major department store. All day long, she received returned merchandise and gave refunds or store credit. Many customers were aggressive and made outrageous requests—such as full refunds for old, broken merchandise. Martha had no outlet for the anger that this behavior inspired, so she would come home at night feeling drained and hungry. She'd head right to the refrigerator and eat whatever was quick and filling: ice cream, cookie dough, leftovers. It didn't matter what type of food it was as long as it could be consumed quickly and

easily. Martha was vainly attempting to quell the caul-
dron of anger deep within her by filling it with food.

— Another client, Jan, was quite aware of the anger
brewing within her when she entered therapy. However,
she expressed trepidation about releasing this anger for
fear that she'd completely lose control. This poised,
well-dressed woman told me, "I just know if I let out this
anger, I'll do something radical, like smash down all the
walls in my house or break things."

Years and years of repressed anger had been stopped
up by a 50-pound wall of fat on her body. But, as Jan let
out her steam bit by bit over the months, she was able to
maintain control of her emotions. And as the steam of
anger was released, so too were the excess pounds and
overactive appetite.

Tension

Tension is the physical manifestation of stress. Stress itself
really doesn't hurt us, because it is caused by forces outside of us.
It is our *internalization* of the stress, in the form of tension and
anxiety, that's the problem. "Stress management" has always
seemed like a contradictory term to me, because we can't control
the stress in the world. We can only control or manage our internal response to stress: tension. Trying to control something
uncontrollable, such as stress, only creates more tension. Besides,
a lot of stressful situations result in positive outcomes, such as
buying a home, celebrating the holidays, and getting married. In
addition, what causes tension in some people does not cause it in

others. Our beliefs about, and interpretation of, a situation cause tension in our bodies—and also determine the *amount* of tension we experience.

Renowned philosopher and author Rollo May argues against using the word *stress* to describe both cause and effect—that is, he says that it's a mistake to use *stress* synonymously with the word *anxiety* because the former is the cause and the latter is the effect. May writes, "If we use stress as a synonym for anxiety, we cannot distinguish between the different (underlying) emotions" such as fear, grief, and anger.

That's why I prefer to use the word *tension,* because this is the most identifiable outcome of stressors. The tension reaction leads to overeating, as we seek to relax and unwind with the comfort of ice cream, cookies, hamburgers, or even "health foods."

Tension is also a major factor leading to compulsive overeating due to psychological and physical forces. New studies point to brain chemistry changes in response to tension. These changes increase our cravings for certain foods, especially those loaded with carbohydrates. A high-carbohydrate diet can be good for you, but only if it's composed of low-fat foods eaten in moderation. Tension often triggers the consumption of high-fat carbohydrates such as chocolate, cake, cookies, breads, or bingeing on huge quantities of "fat-free" carbohydrates such as rice cakes or muffins.

Several well-conducted studies (Strober; Cattanach; Mynors-Wallis; and Terr) have looked at the connection between "stressful life events," including child abuse, and overeating. These studies have concluded that people who binge-eat or who have clinically diagnosed eating disorders, have experienced significantly more life traumas and "stressors" than people who don't binge-eat. The researchers have also concluded that eating is the chief tension-management tool used by these trauma survivors.

Dr. Sarah Leibowitz of Rockefeller University has studied the relationship between tension and brain chemistry for a number of years and has made some fascinating discoveries (Marano, 1993). Leibowitz identified brain and hormonal substances influencing our cravings for carbohydrates, one of which was *cortisol,* a hormone that the brain produces to anesthetize pain; Interestingly enough, Leibowitz found that the adrenal glands produce excess cortisol in response to tension. The cortisol then stimulates production of a brain chemical called *neuropeptide Y,* identified by Leibowitz as being a chief factor in turning our carbohydrate cravings on and off.

In other words, tension makes us crave carbohydrates. And if we consume excess carbohydrates, especially the high-fat variety, it's converted into body fat. Even worse, reports Leibowitz, these tension-induced chemicals also make the body hang on to the new body fat we produce. So tension not only creates an overactive appetite—it makes it more difficult to lose body fat!

Another researcher, Judith Wurtman of MIT, has written many journal articles and books on the relationship between the brain chemical *serotonin* and carbohydrate cravings. Serotonin is a "messenger" chemical (a neurotransmitter) that is largely responsible for affecting our moods and energy levels. When serotonin levels are low, so too is our energy and mood. Wurtman found that carbohydrates trigger a chemical reaction that increases serotonin production.

Since tension depletes and lowers serotonin levels, when you're experiencing prolonged tension, your carbohydrate cravings may be increased.

An interesting study from Yale University found a disturbing relationship between tension and "potbellies" (Bricklin, M., 1993). Yale researchers Marielle Rebufe-Scrive, Ph.D., and Judith Rodin,

Ph.D., concluded from extensive work with animal and human subjects that tension increases the amount of body fat, especially around the midsection. Abdominal fat is associated with increased risk for heart disease, stroke, and diabetes in both men and women.

In light of these facts, before I turn to a discussion of the final FATS feeling, Shame, I'm going to discuss some ways to diminish the health risks mentioned above.

Three Ways to Stop Procrastinating and Start Exercising

Exercise increases the amount of serotonin your brain produces (Chaouloff, F., et al., 1989), which lessens your carbohydrate cravings, elevates your energy level, and brightens your mood. Exercise is the best tension-management tool and body-fat burner there is, yet many of us resist it. Why?

I've learned that exercise is only effective if you stick with it—and the only way to stick to something is if it fits your personality. I'm a person who needs lots of intellectual stimulation. I love reading and having great conversations. So I found an exercise program that allowed me to read while working out: the StairMaster! You can also read while pedaling on a stationary bicycle. Or, you can watch television while jogging on a treadmill.

My favorite exercise, though, is jogging outside in nature. I often drive to areas with beautiful scenery so that I can jog and sightsee simultaneously. In this way, I get the benefit of fresh air, sunshine (hopefully), and a feast for my eyes. On one jogging expedition at the beach, I happened upon a large group of people who were "oohing" and "ahhing." There, just off the coast, was a large whale, jumping in and out of the water. If I hadn't been jogging, I might have missed one of the greatest scenes of my life!

I've learned how to trick myself into exercising, and it's worked well for several years. I still don't love to exercise, but then I don't expect to. Here are the tricks that work for me, and which have worked well for my clients and workshop attendees:

1. *See exercise as part of your daily routine, not something that is optional.* Why? Because when you ask yourself, "Do I exercise today, or don't I?", you might very well decide that you don't have enough time. Instead, you've got to go to the bank, the store, the office, home—just about anyplace where you can avoid exercising. The minute you allow yourself to engage in a mental argument— "Do I exercise or don't I?"—you increase the odds that you won't exercise.

So, stop looking at exercise as an optional activity. It's not! It's a necessity for a long, healthy life (in conjunction with weight control and tension management, of course).

You might try writing down your exercise schedule in ink on your calendar, just as you do your other important appointments and meetings that you don't want to miss. Figure out a realistic schedule for exercising several times a week, and then stick to it. Never cancel your exercise session—if something unavoidable comes up, simply reschedule your session within the same day.

2. *Pair exercise with something you enjoy.* This really works for me. I make sure I always have something interesting to read—a new magazine, a book, or an intriguing newspaper article. Then, I don't let myself read it unless I'm exercising. As I mentioned before, I get really bored exercising unless my mind is also being stimulated. As I mentioned above, my Stairmaster allows me the flexibility of reading while I'm working out. I've found that health-oriented magazines such as *Prevention, Fitness,*

and *Shape* are very motivational while working out.

Be patient with yourself if you're just starting an exercise routine. If your body is large, I urge you to consider joining a gym that offers workout classes especially designed for larger bodies. Many of the all-women gyms offer these classes. The instructors are usually women who have lost a great deal of weight, and who understand the challenges of being heavy. Therefore, the exercise routines are geared toward your special needs and limitations. In these classes, you'll find that you'll be surrounded by a support system that is extremely motivating. You'll also feel more comfortable being in sweats or leotards around other women, especially others who are also trying to lose a lot of weight.

In addition to a more strenuous aerobic workout, I also do a mini-weight workout every other day. Like most exercise routines, working with weights is not my idea of great fun, but the results are definitely worth it. Thanks to this weight training, my muscles feel more toned and shaped than they have in my whole life.

To motivate myself, I do my weight workouts while listening to my favorite radio talk show. If my schedule doesn't allow me to workout at that time, I tape the show to listen to it later. If I were working out at a gym or jogging somewhere, I'd take the tape and a cassette player with me.

Many of my clients have paired watching television with workouts on treadmills and stationary bicycles. If, for example, you videotape your favorite soap opera while you're at work every day, don't allow yourself to watch it unless you exercise.

I find it interesting that a survey (Neergaard, 1993) showed that 64 percent of 1,018 sedentary Americans polled said they would like to exercise but don't have enough time. In the same survey—with the same people—84 percent reported watching at least three hours of television a week. The surveyors concluded, as you may have guessed, that the solution was to exercise while they watched television.

3. *Do the "15-minute Trick."* Here's another great motivator, especially for those days when you just don't want to exercise. Tell yourself, "I'll only work out for 15 minutes. If I feel like stopping at the end of those 15 minutes, I will." Nine times out of ten, you'll keep going once you get to the end of your allotted time. After all, you've already gone to the trouble of putting on your workout clothes and shoes. But, if you really want to stop after 15 minutes, allow yourself to do so.

Shame

Shame is the final FATS emotion that can trigger overeating. Shame is self-blame, guilt, self-doubt, depression, and low self-esteem all wrapped up in one. Think of the little dog who has been beaten, yelled at, and ignored. She keeps her head down low and her tail between her legs, sending a message that she hopes will protect her from further injury: "I'm not a threat; I'm weak. Please don't hurt me. I'm sad, and I'm sorry."

I've worked with many clients who have exhibited these signs of shame. Shame starts in childhood, when the little girl blames herself for the neglect or abuse she receives. Instead of being angry at the abuser, she assumes that she must have caused the adult to be angry. She internalizes the anger, turning it toward herself instead of toward its rightful owner.

Since she blames herself, she feels guilt and shame. As I mentioned earlier, sexual abuse and rape survivors often mentally beat themselves up for "causing" the incident, a lie perpetuated by the sexual offender who convinces her that she "asked for it." Her self-doubt ("Did I cause him to do this to me?") is further compounded by shame over any normal physical reactions of sexual arousal. She's horrified that her body would betray her like this!

Sexual abuse survivors usually feel damaged or broken. My client Corrine, who was repeatedly raped by her father, was shocked when she got pregnant in her early 30s. "Deep down, I thought my uterus and womb were broken by the abuse," she told me.

In a study of 500 adolescents, researchers Cavaiola and Schiff (1989) found that 150 of the teenagers had been physically or sexually abused. These 150 teens had significantly lower self-esteem levels compared to the teens who hadn't been abused, regardless of what type of abuse the girl or boy had suffered.

Another study of 78 eating-disordered females (Oppenheimer, 1985) concluded: "Frequently the sexually molested subject has feelings of inferiority or disgust about her own femininity and sexuality. These may come to be entangled with concern about her body weight, shape, and size."

Shame triggers eating for a number of reasons. The woman experiencing this emotion eats for comfort, companionship, and recreation because she avoids social situations that normally fill these human needs. She isolates herself from others, judging herself as unworthy. "No one would like me anyway," she may assume.

Sadly, as the woman gains weight, the shame increases. Researchers (Martin, et al.,1988) administered self-esteem tests to 550 girls between the ages of 14 and 16. They found strong correlations between weight and self-esteem, concluding that "as weight increased, self-esteem decreased."

When she eats so much that her body becomes morbidly

obese, the woman finds that people treat her fat body with contempt.

"I'll be out shopping and someone will say to me, 'What a fat pig,'" my client Jody told me. "Do they think that just because I'm fat, I don't have any feelings?" Jody finds that she eats more on days when people are cruel to her.

Turning FATS Around

We've looked at different situations and feelings that trigger the appetite for food. We've also touched on several solutions. At this point, our goal is to become more aware and honest with ourselves.

When you're hungry, it's vital that you resist the impulse to automatically reach for food. Instead, ask yourself: "Could I be feeling Fear, Anger, Tension, or Shame?" Just by asking yourself that question, you'll feel more in control of your eating. In fact, in many instances, this question can eliminate the emotional hunger—or at least reduce it to a manageable size.

The affirmations and visualization tools in the next chapter are the same ones I've used in my own healing, as well as with my clients and workshop attendees. Please take the time to put my suggestions into action. They really do work, but first you have to make the effort to implement them into your life. There is no easier way to permanently lessen your appetite for food—no magic pill, powder, or food combination.

chapter eleven

BREAKING THE POUND/PAIN CYCLE

*"So Jesus said to them, Because you have so little
faith. I tell you the truth, if you have faith as small
as a mustard seed, you can say to this mountain,
'Move from here to there' and it will move.
Nothing will be impossible for you."*
— Matthew 17:20

You've come so far already, and the best is yet to come. By changing your thinking, you'll find that your body is changing. That means that your appetite will lessen and your body fat will drop away. You'll no longer need the defenses that food and fat give you. It's time to tear down your walls—you're no longer in danger; you're safe.

As a child, you weren't responsible for what happened to you—the adult or adolescent who harmed you was at fault. (As you've probably noticed, this is a point that I have never tired of repeating throughout this book.) So, the first thing I'd like you to do is call up a clear mental picture of yourself as a little girl or adolescent, around the time that you were first abused, neglected, injured, or hurt.

Now, please give that little girl a big mental hug. Tell her that it's okay, that it wasn't her fault, that you love her. Tell her not to worry. Most of all, tell her to forgive herself, since she didn't do anything wrong.

Whenever you feel the first FATS feeling, "Fear," I want you to immediately hug that little girl deep inside you. Tell her she's safe. Tell her you care.

Now you're starting to transform the FATS feelings from Fear, Anger, Tension, and Shame . . . into Forgiving, Accepting, and Trusting one's Self. By giving your inner little girl lots of hugs, praise, encouragement, and love, you're essentially "re-parenting" yourself. You're being the mother and father that you needed when you were growing up. I really like this saying, and think that it really hits the mark: "It's never too late to have a happy childhood."

Whenever you feel Fear, Anger, Tension, or Shame, immediately declare this affirmation: *"I Forgive, Accept, and Trust my Self."* Say it over and over, allowing the strength of the conviction to conquer feelings of insecurity.

That statement is the most important concept behind your healing process. Please write the phrase on a card or piece of paper, and look at it often. You may want to tape the card to your bathroom mirror, your refrigerator, or your computer monitor.

What follows are additional affirmations to use as part of your healing. Earlier in the book, I described how I used these affirmations to heal my own situation, and how my clients made affirmation tapes to achieve remarkable progress. I urge you to do the same.

Affirmations

I am a good person.

Today, I release my pain.

Right now, good is happening to me.

I love the little girl inside of me.

I am made in the image and likeness of God.

I take very good care of myself.

I deserve the best that life has to offer.

I am whole and complete.

I give myself permission to take care of my needs.

I enjoy taking care of myself.

God wants me to be content.

My family benefits when I'm happy.

I ask for, and accept, help from others.

I am strong.

I believe in my dreams.

I can achieve whatever I can see.

Today, I am taking steps toward realizing my dreams.

If it is going to be, it is up to me.

I accept challenges.

I am creative.

I am a good problem-solver.

I have common sense.

I am a successful person.

I manage my finances well.

I surround myself with loving people.

I expect, and deserve, fulfilling relationships.

I attract happy, healthy people into my life.

I am investing in my future.

It feels good to take care of myself.

I reward myself for my efforts.
This is the perfect time to work toward my dreams.
I trust my judgment and inner voice.
I am intuitive.
I follow the path that is best for me.
I express my feelings.
It is okay for me to be honest.
I am always in good company.
I am safe and secure.
I expect the best to happen.
Good things are happening to me right now.
I am planting seeds for my future.
I enjoy my successes.
I accept compliments.
I take calculated risks.
I am making a wish list, and it is being fulfilled.
All of my dreams are coming true.
Life is a wonderful journey.
My body is perfect, healthy, and whole.

In her inspirational classic, *You Can Heal Your Life*, Louise Hay discusses the power of affirmations as a way of letting go of addictions to problems of all kinds. She writes:

> I say to clients, "There must be a need in you for this con-
> dition, or you wouldn't have it. Let's go back a step and work
> on the WILLINGNESS TO RELEASE THE NEED. When the
> need is gone, you will have no desire for the cigarette or the
> overeating or the negative pattern.
> One of the first affirmations to use is: *"I am willing to
> release the NEED for the resistance, or the headache, or the*

constipation, or the excess weight, or the lack of money or whatever." Say: *"I am willing to release the need for . . ."* If you're resisting at this point, then your other affirmations cannot work.

I heartily agree with Louise Hay's contention that when you feel the overwhelming urge to binge-eat, it's important to look underneath it and examine the motives driving you to feel this hunger. Instead of heading to the cupboard or refrigerator, pause one brief moment and ask yourself, "Am I running away from a troubling thought or emotion?" Just by posing this question, you'll regain enough awareness and composure to put the brakes on a potential binge situation before it accelerates.

The Power of Visualization

I've always been an advocate of the power of visualization, and I've used it to achieve incredible success in my own life. However, I don't think that visualization works as a result of any magic or divine intervention—I believe it works because, if you can picture achieving a goal, you'll keep working at it until you actually do so.

Before I was a published author, I visualized my book appearing in print. My mental image of my published book was in graphic detail; I even decided that Bantam, a major publisher, would buy my manuscript.

To make my visualization as real as possible, I cut the little Bantam logo—a red rooster—off the pages and covers of every Bantam paperback I owned. I taped these little roosters all over the place: on my bathroom mirror, on the refrigerator door, and on the dashboard of my car. During my daily meditations, I could picture my book in the bookstore with my name printed on the book spine, right below the Bantam rooster.

I hung on to this image until it felt like second nature to me. I trusted that if I worked hard enough, I would be published by Bantam just as I'd envisioned. Well, my first book—*My Kids Don't Live with Me Anymore: Coping with the Custody Crisis*—was almost bought by Bantam, but they decided at the last minute that since they already had a book on child custody in print, they'd pass on my project.

Another book I wrote was sold by auction through my literary agent, and Bantam was one of the publishers making a bid. Alas, they bid much lower than Harper & Row, who ended up publishing *The Yo-Yo Syndrome Diet*. (It was later updated and republished by Hay House as *The Yo-Yo Diet Syndrome.*)

The third time was the charm, however. During my book tour for *The Yo-Yo Syndrome Diet*, most of the talk-show hosts and studio audiences wanted to discuss chocolate and chocoholism. My philosophy about chocoholism is twofold: Chocolate cravings stem from an unbalanced diet and/or psychological issues (many of which have been addressed in this book); and second, if you totally abstain from chocolate, you'll feel deprived and end up overindulging in a chocolate-eating binge. What's better is to eat a small amount of low-fat chocolate in moderation. That was a topic I'd covered only briefly in the book, so I decided to write a third book, *The Chocoholic's Dream Diet*.

Bantam was the first bidder on that book, and I jumped at the chance to be published by them! When the book came out, I saw it for the first time in a bookstore. There it was, just like I'd visualized it for four years, with my name on the spine and the little red rooster right above it. That was a real thrill—and confirmed the power of visualization to me. I'd hung on to the picture in my mind until it came true!

One of the best books on the topic of visualization is *Positive Imaging* by Norman Vincent Peale. Actually, all of his books are wonderful, but this particular one is very focused on the topic. I've recommended it to many of my clients.

As I mentioned earlier, I also found Louise Hay's *You Can Heal Your Life* extremely valuable in examining the destructive pictures that I held in mind with respect to money and relationships. With the help of her book, I "edited" my images concerning my right to have financial and love-life successes. It helped me tremendously in creating the fulfilling life I have today.

See Yourself Thin: The Case of Elaine

Elaine was a woman who started psychotherapy with me in order to lose weight. She was a sexy woman who took good care of her hair and complexion, and although her factory job required her to dress in jeans and T-shirts, she always looked well groomed. She told me during our first session that she was the only woman working in an otherwise all-male department.

Elaine, who stood 5'7" and weighed 235 pounds, had joined four weight-loss programs the year before she came to me. She easily lost weight with each dieting attempt, but would always skid to a plateau halt as soon as she neared the 200-pound mark.

"I never get under 200 pounds," she firmly announced. Her words, and the way she said them, told me that Elaine's weight plateau was a decision she'd made. But I didn't discuss this with her right away. She wouldn't have believed me.

Instead, Elaine participated in my traditional psychotherapy sessions with an emphasis on weight loss. It was no surprise to me that her weight started dropping off like the fur a cat sheds during the summer. Her weight dropped: 230, 225, 220—down, down, down it went. Each week we'd deal with painful experiences from her present and past—uncovering and releasing the pain—and along with it, the excess pounds.

Then it happened. She reached 202 pounds and stayed right there. For a month and a half, her weight fluctuated between 201 and 204. Finally, when we both feared she'd abandon her weight-loss efforts altogether, I helped her acknowledge what she needed to see: Elaine couldn't get below 200 pounds because she couldn't see herself under that weight.

First, I asked Elaine to close her eyes to block out any distractions. I asked her to picture herself standing on her bathroom scale. We made the image vivid, and I asked her to describe everything she "saw" in her visualization. She described that she was wearing underwear, that her feet felt a little cold as she stepped on the metal scale, and that the toilet paper roll was almost empty.

Then I asked her to look at the number on the scale. What did it say?

"202 pounds," she replied.

"Okay, I'd like you to picture that number changing. Can you imagine the scale saying 201?"

"Yes," said Elaine.

"Good. Now can you change the number to 200?"

After a moment, Elaine said, "Yes, it's 200 now."

"All right. Now let's keep going. I'd like you to see

199 on the scale."

Silence.

"Can you see 199 on the scale, Elaine?" I asked.

"Um . . . well, not really," Elaine struggled to explain. Her eyes were now wide open as she told me, "Every time I see 199, it changes instantaneously back to 200!"

"Okay," I reassured her, "let's try again. After you close your eyes, I'd like to ask you to take some really deep breaths . . ."

We worked on her mental image for the remainder of our hour together. But it took another session before Elaine was able to see—and hold on to—an image of herself below 200 pounds. Once she was able to "lock on" to a firm, steady mental picture of the scale reaching 199, her actual weight followed suit. At the next week's session, Elaine hugged me and showed me a Polaroid snapshot she'd taken while standing on her bathroom scale. The photo revealed a pair of bare feet and red LED numbers flashing 199!

"Just like in our visualization!" Elaine exclaimed happily.

You see, until Elaine could actually visualize her weight below 200 pounds, she couldn't achieve that goal. She believed that she was destined to plateau at 200 pounds, and she unconsciously made this belief come true. Again, the power of visualization isn't the product of some voodoo magic—it just shows the impact our decisions make on our lives.

Elaine had decided with absolute certainty that she couldn't get below 200 pounds. Every time she'd get close, she'd think, *What's the use?* and would slacken off in her weight-loss efforts. She'd skip going to the gym, she'd use extra blue cheese salad dressing instead of low-fat—and sure enough her weight would "plateau," as if by magic.

It didn't help that one of her diet club "counselors" (actually, an untrained salesperson wearing a white laboratory coat) had reinforced Elaine's belief in her 200-pound plateau. "It's your set-point," the counselor had told Elaine. "It's probably a genetically programmed weight that your body is comfortable at." That statement set into concrete Elaine's belief that she'd never reach her goal weight of 150 pounds.

A good analogy would be if someone was told her entire life, "You'll never succeed, and you'll never make anything of yourself." Suppose that person wanted to get a college degree but held on to the belief that she'd always fail at any goal she attempted. If she finished all her college classes except one, she'd be very close to her goal. But if she did not really believe that she deserved to attain it, she would not allow herself to succeed. This is the kind of person who would suddenly find something "more important" to do—like get married, get a job, move away, or have a baby—and would seem to have a perfectly rational reason for falling short of her goal. She would rationalize to herself and others why she couldn't finish her degree.

Elaine's set-point theory—"I'm genetically programmed to have a weight plateau at 200 pounds"— was exactly the same thing. She'd get close to achieving her goal and then would stop short. However, when I helped her alter this mental picture, her expectations changed. And so did her behavior.

You Deserve to Have the Body You Desire

One of the barriers Elaine encountered was the sense that she didn't deserve to achieve her weight-loss goal. After her weight dropped down to about 180, Elaine began to fear that she'd put the weight back on. Why was this so? Since every extra pound on her body was equal to a pound of pain, we began exploring the issues that made her think she didn't deserve a normal-weight body.

As I mentioned before, Elaine's job thrust her in the middle of an all-male department. We discussed her feelings about male attention, and right away it was evident that this was an issue for Elaine. It turned out that she was afraid of men's admiring glances and compliments about her improved figure.

Elaine was one of those naturally sexy women who just oozed charisma and sex appeal, in spite of the excess weight she carried. She was like a Mae West with auburn hair—someone with bedroom eyes and a throaty voice—and guys just went nuts for her. That petrified her.

We discovered that she felt guilty about her natural power to attract men. To get to the basis for this guilt, I asked Elaine to remember all the times she'd felt this way. Back, back, we went, uncovering layers of years when Elaine recalled that other women were jealous of her for getting all the boyfriends she wanted. Still, that wasn't the root of her guilt.

What we eventually uncovered stemmed from her childhood. Elaine and her father had had a close bond when she was a child, and they would go out for errands and day trips together, and her father treated her like she was a grown-up. He'd talk to her about all sorts of things: his work, his dreams, and his girlfriends.

"His girlfriends?" I interrupted Elaine's recounting of her childhood. "But weren't your parents married for 40 years when he passed away?"

"Yes, but he had mistresses throughout their marriage. I don't know if my mom ever knew about the affairs, but my Dad told me about each and every one of them," Elaine said with a grimace. "In fact, he used to take me along on his 'dates.' I guess I was his excuse to get out of the house."

Elaine and I discovered that, although she had been flattered to be Daddy's "special friend" and confidante, it was a burden that she wasn't emotionally prepared to handle. She remembered that each girlfriend she met was always the same "type": voluptuous with a big hairdo. The three of them would eat at a restaurant, go to a movie, or go to the girlfriend's home. These women would then attempt to win Elaine's affection and approval, but she felt nothing but contempt and pity for them. They were, after all, threatening her mother's place in her life.

Elaine never told anyone about her father's affairs. When she grew up and found her own body mimicking the voluptuous figures of her Dad's girlfriends, Elaine was horrified. She was even more appalled when men began asking her out regularly. That's when she started putting the extra weight on.

Whenever Elaine's weight would drop at all, her naturally sexy figure and personality would begin to shine through. Men would start to notice her, and her guilt and fear would be triggered. She was especially aghast that most of the men at work were married, yet they would still make passes at her thinning body.

"It's like I'm one of Dad's girlfriends," she finally admitted to herself. As soon as she saw the root of her pound/pain link, we were able to work through and release it. Elaine understood why she felt undeserving of a thin, normal-weight body. She could see why she feared male attention, and why she felt guilty about being attractive. She also changed her mental image of her weight, so now she could picture "150" on her bathroom scale.

Within two months, the 150-pound goal was a reality. Elaine no longer feared regaining the weight, and she'd learned to be assertive when dealing with the attention directed her way by men. Inappropriate advances, in the form of sexual harassment, were dealt with through normal company channels. More harmless types of male attention she simply shrugged off as a normal part of female life. Elaine learned that "nice" girls do get whistled at. And sometimes they even enjoy it.

What Is Your Self-Image?

There's an old saying that I believe bears a lot of truth: "God wouldn't give us the ability to dream, without also giving us the ability to make the dream come true." I think we all know, deep inside, what our God-given dream is and who our self is, in all respects: looks, lifestyle, occupation, and personality.

But what would your "fantasy you" be like? That is, if you could change yourself and become any "you" you wanted, what would you be like? What would you look like? How would you act? What kind of job would you aspire to? What kind of home life would you have?

This fantasy is your "blueprint" to your God-given dream life. You can choose to completely remodel your present situation, or just do a little rearranging. I used my blueprint to make some major overhauls, and those actions on my part saved my life.

When you're not fulfilling your mission or purpose, you experience pressures and discomfort. Something just feels wrong. For me, I had this sense of time urgency—the fear that I'd die before I accomplished what I was destined to do. Believe me, this emotional distress caused me a lot of stomachaches; the pressure of not following my blueprint was eating away at me!

When I got on the right track and started following my mental plan—to be a psychologist and a bestselling author, to have an attractive figure and a great relationship and live on the water— it seemed like I was preparing to climb Mt. Everest. I wasn't sure I was going to get to the top, but I sure needed to try!

Something that really helped me achieve my goals, besides my daily affirmations and visualizations, was writing down all my wishes. One of my professors, a woman whom I admired, gave my class an assignment to write down every one of our wildest dreams. I wrote everything I could think of—like a kid given free reign at a toy store. I put the list away and didn't think about it further.

About three years later, I found the list among some papers, and guess what? I had accomplished *everything* on the list—from an exotic vacation, to the car I owned, to graduating, to being a published author, to my improved relationship with my two sons. Everything in my life reflected what I had written on that "wish" list.

Research on the writing-out of goals has confirmed the power and effectiveness of this practice. There's something about the physical act of writing, and then seeing those words on paper, that activates more brain cells than ordinary thinking does. The goals become inscribed in your brain, and your actions reflect your expectation: "I will achieve my goals."

I know that making changes in your life is difficult, painful even. I traveled a long, hard journey myself, and many times I felt discouraged and considered giving up. But always, this pressure deep inside of me kept pushing me, pushing me. That pressure was God, urging me to fulfill His mission, purpose, and plan—something He wants all of us to do.

As your pressure is eased—because you're following your true path—your appetite for food will naturally lessen. As you lose weight, you'll find that this change in your body and figure will inspire new experiences, some of them stressful, but many of them pleasant.

It's very likely that as you lose your pounds of pain, your relationships will evolve and grow, too. You'll be like a room that has been closed for years, and is suddenly opened to the sunlight and fresh air. The light will reveal some dusting, cleaning, and repairs that are needed, but it will also attract many beautiful sights, experiences, and beings. You might also find that the light will repel some people in your life who desperately cling to negative beliefs. You may find that you need to say good-bye to those people who insist on staying in the "dark," as they will only bring you down.

As you stop overeating, you may also become painfully aware of life situations that trouble you. Food, for so many, is used as a means of blocking out conscious awareness of troubling marriages, unfulfilling jobs, financial difficulties and family strife. When you remove the excess food from your life, you become more aware of *everything* around you, both good and bad. Naturally there will be times when you will be tempted to dive right back into overeating, but the best way to avoid reverting to old habits is to be truthful with yourself about your motives.

As you begin to realize that you're overindulging, ask yourself the important question: "*Why* am I eating this?" As I've mentioned several times before, the sheer act of questioning yourself will help jolt you back into awareness. You automatically gain more control over your actions when you're truthful with yourself about your motives and intentions.

Remember, every time you put food in your mouth, you're deciding what size body you'll have. When you choose to eat a lot—especially high-fat food—you're choosing a high-fat figure. The day you stop blaming your spouse, your children, your schedule, your job, your finances, your genetics, your thyroid, your metabolism, or your age for your weight—is the day you'll begin choosing to lose the weight and keep it off.

I understand how tempting it is to blame external circumstances for your overweight body. I had the perfect excuse to stay fat: I had borne two children and had come from a long line of overweight women. However, I chose not to accept those excuses as my reality. And I'm happy to report that, in recent years, my mother and my maternal grandmother have also decided to adopt fat-free lifestyles. We rejected blame, and accepted responsibility for choosing our body sizes!

The vexing dilemma behind this wonderful choice is the knowledge that you—and only you—are in the driver's seat when it comes to the number of pounds you carry on your body. But here's a question for you: Is the fact that you're completely responsible for your weight a burdensome responsibility or a joyful choice? The former is a heavy, ponderous thought, while the latter is a light, carefree idea. And since our thoughts reflect our body weight, it's best to look at the situation as an *opportunity*.

You are free to choose!

chapter twelve

CAN THERAPY HELP ME?

*"Of all the destructive words in common use,
surely one of the most powerful is the word 'impossible.'
More people may have failed by using that one word
than almost any other in the English language."*
— Norman Vincent Peale

I believe that all abuse survivors, especially sexual abuse survivors, can benefit from *appropriate psychotherapy*. If you're thinking about going to a therapist, here are the benefits you can expect to reap:

- Feeling more accepting of yourself
- Liking yourself a lot more
- Sleeping more soundly at night, with fewer nightmares and/or bouts of insomnia
- Less compulsion to overeat, overdrink, or use drugs
- Fewer relationship difficulties, such as arguments, irritability
- Better skills with respect to choosing romantic partners
- More ability to concentrate and focus

- Increased motivation to take good care of yourself
- Feeling more organized
- Feeling more relaxed about yourself and life in general
- Better relationships with your children.
- Better understanding or memory of your childhood.
- Being more attuned to the feelings of friends and relatives

These are just some of the benefits of *appropriate* psychotherapy, which is a key term encompassing these essential elements:

1. The therapist must be experienced in treating sexual abuse survivors. More and more psychotherapists are specializing in this area because there is so much knowledge and information to absorb in order to effectively treat abused clients.

You can identify a trained sexual abuse therapist in a number of different ways. If you belong to a support group, other members can make recommendations. In addition, *Yellow Pages* advertisements for psychologists often mention key phrases such as "Women's Issues," "Abuse Survivors," "Trauma Recovery," or "Adult Children of Alcoholics" (even if your parent wasn't an alcoholic, therapists in that field are experienced in dealing with abuse issues).

Be sure to choose a licensed psychotherapist with at least a master's degree in psychology or social work. This graduate education provides vital training for therapists, and helps them gain maturity and skills not afforded at the undergraduate level.

Important: Never allow an unqualified person who calls him- or herself a "counselor" (a title used by many of the commercial weight-loss programs) to delve deeply into your psychological issues. These untrained persons—who may very well be concerned people with good intentions—can do a lot more harm than good. They simply don't have the skills, training, or experience to separate their own issues from their clients'.

2. When meeting with the therapist for the first time, make sure you feel comfortable enough to be completely open with her (or him). Ask yourself during the first session: Do I like this therapist as a person? Do I feel I can truly open up? Are her words nonjudgmental? Will she give me advice and direction, or will she allow me to make my own choices and decisions?

Don't worry about offending the therapist if you choose not to return for further sessions. Therapists know that they can't be everything to everybody, and that some clients won't connect well with them. Therapists don't take it personally when a client "shops around" and then decides to be treated by a different person. Besides, if the therapist *does* take it personally, this is a clear indication that you would not want to be "helped" by this person in the first place.

3. When it comes to treating sexual abuse, there are three types of therapists:

a. The first type includes those who are inexperienced with sexual abuse, and either downplay the significance of this trauma, avoid delving into this issue with the client at all, or give unhealthful advice. Ask your potential therapist how many cases of sexual abuse she has dealt with, and then listen to how she answers this question.

b. The second type believes that all women with eating disorders have been sexually abused. Beware of this type of therapist! These people have a cookie-cutter, simplistic philosophy and try to make all their clients conform to the same diagnosis and treatment. They are also the therapists responsible for creating the "false memory" hysteria—they actually encourage clients to say they remember being molested by their parents. This situation, as you can imagine, creates heartache and disruption within families—sometimes permanently. You can spot a "cookie-cutter" therapist pretty easily. She will *tell you*—as if it's an indisputable fact—that you've been sexually abused even if you've never brought up the subject. If this happens, find another therapist immediately.

c. The third type is experienced and open-minded, someone who will really listen to you. She will help you deal with the emotional pain connected to genuine memories of abuse, but she won't prompt you in any way. Also, she will emotionally support you while you tell her—and yourself—what happened. This is the best therapist for you. Don't quit until you find her.

Many female sexual abuse survivors choose same-sex therapists because they feel awkward discussing embarrassing details about the abuse with male therapists. I have met and worked with many highly qualified male therapists who work very effectively with sexual abuse survivors. However, these men are aware that female abuse survivors might shun them, and they're not offended by being passed over for a woman.

In the two all-women psychiatric hospitals where I was an administrator, 95 percent of the staff was made up of women. The few men on staff tried their best to help their patients regain some trust in men, but there were still some unavoidable problems, such as the time a male nurse was in the unisex rest room, standing and urinating like a normal man. One of the female patients accidentally opened the door to the single-stall rest room and saw the male nurse's penis. She practically collapsed out of surprise and embarrassment, and the incident triggered a lot of issues surrounding her original sexual abuse episodes.

As far as financial issues are concerned, most health insurance policies cover part of the outpatient therapy cost. Also, the majority of therapists will work with you to create a fee schedule that fits your budget. These therapists know that if therapy costs so much that it creates money problems, you won't feel any better about your life. They want you to come in for treatment, and they'll slash the price of therapy sessions to help you. My personal policy was to offer free therapy to two patients, per caseload. It was my way of giving back, to help people who otherwise couldn't afford therapy. And, believe me, they received the same quality of therapy as someone paying full price.

What about outpatient therapy versus checking into a psychiatric hospital for a couple of weeks? Well, most insurance companies insist that before they'll cover the cost of inpatient psychiatric care, you first try outpatient therapy. I agree. I think that with any type of health care—whether for physical or mental ailments, it's best to try the least intrusive method first.

Usually, people who need inpatient care are:

- suicidal, and in need of 24-hour supervision just to stay alive;
- delusional, hallucinating, or dissociating;
- those whose home and/or work life is perpetually keeping them sick, and who literally need to remove themselves from an unhealthy environment in order to get better.

There are advantages to receiving inpatient care over outpatient therapy, especially for sexual abuse survivors who compulsively overeat. Let's say, for example, that you're trying to work through intense memories of sexual abuse by seeing your therapist on your lunch hour. You're going to hold back a lot of your emotions just to maintain your composure so you can return to work without mascara running down your cheekbones from crying so much. In a psychiatric hospital, you don't have to worry about your job or your makeup. You can dive right into your emotions and stay with them until the issues are resolved.

Another benefit to inpatient care is that psychiatric hospitals accustomed to dealing with abuse and overeating issues will monitor your eating. While this may trigger rebellion in patients with control issues connected to eating, it will also serve a positive purpose. If that food has been keeping a lid on your memories and emotions, your feelings will be closer to the surface if you're not compulsively overeating. So, the hospital environment that monitors your eating may help you access your important thoughts and feelings about the abuse.

You can also give yourself this intense type of treatment on an outpatient basis by combining psychotherapy with attendance at Overeaters Anonymous (OA) meetings, where you will be assigned a sponsor. This type of combination therapy will help you access many abuse-related memories and thoughts.

The OA meetings and sponsor will help you monitor your eating and abstain from any "binge foods" (usually those with refined white flour or processed sugar). By regulating your eating, you'll be more apt to focus on profound abuse issues while seeing your psychotherapist.

It's important to attend OA meetings that are compatible with your personality and lifestyle. I recommend attending three different OA meetings before choosing one that you'll attend regularly. Look for a meeting with group members who are healthy, and not just sitting around making excuses or feeling sorry for themselves. A good way to assess the situation is to discern if at least three or four group members have abstained from compulsive overeating for more than one year (long-term abstainers announce their success at the beginning of meetings).

At the end of the meeting, sponsors will raise their hands. A sponsor is someone whom you will talk to on the phone, or in person, every day. You will tell that person what you plan to eat, as a way of nailing down an eating plan, as opposed to impulsively deciding to overeat. It's frightening in the beginning to approach a sponsor, and many people feel intimidated by the process. Also, some people procrastinate before getting a sponsor, waiting for the "perfect person" to appear. The sponsor relationship really helps compulsive overeaters break out of compulsive overeating. So, take a deep breath and walk up to one of the sponsors, put out your hand, and just say, "I need a sponsor." The sponsor will do all the rest!

It's important to choose a sponsor who has abstained from compulsive overeating for at least one and a half years, preferably longer. Always choose a same-sex sponsor, and don't let anyone tell you otherwise. Male and female issues are just too different for an opposite-sex sponsor to maintain a productive long-term relationship with you.

New and Alternative Therapy Treatments

Eye Movement Desensitization and Reprocessing (EMDR) is a therapeutic method that is particularly effective for trauma recovery. It is a noninvasive method using a series of alternating eye movements, sounds, or hand taps, while the person is focusing upon their traumatic memory. Research has shown that EMDR greatly reduces the emotional impact of trauma. You can find an EMDR specialist by contacting the EMDR Association at: [**www.emdria.com**].

Somatic Experiencing (SE) is another effective method for resolution of traumatic experiences. SE is based on the premise that not only the mind, but also the body, stores frozen memories of the trauma. In a safe environment, facilitated by an SE practitioner, the person focuses on specific areas of their body where these traumatic memories are stored. By doing so, the person slowly and gently melts the frozen memory from the body. The person then enjoys a freer range of emotional and physical flexibility. This gives the trauma survivor true choices about her responses to situations, instead of the automatic responses that so often come from post-traumatic stress disorder, anger, and fear. To find an SE practitioner, contact the Foundation for Human Enrichment at: [**www.traumahealing.com**].

Other Support Systems That Work

Not everyone who undergoes therapy connected to weight loss requires intensive psychotherapy. Some people just need a little support while they change their eating and exercise habits. I've turned away several people from psychotherapy because there really were no clinical issues apparent. These women, who came to me for weight-loss support, were really better off at Weight Watchers—which is exactly where I sent them.

In the absence of a history of abuse, many people successfully lose weight—and keep it off—with the Weight Watchers program. The two things that make this program superior to other diet organizations are: The counselors don't pretend to be psychotherapists, and they offer balanced diets (although some are too high in sodium and artificial sweeteners for my taste).

But on the whole, I believe that Weight Watchers provides appropriate support. This group discusses lifestyle issues without delving into deep psychological issues. They don't use hard-sell or bait-and-switch advertising techniques. They offer group forums where people can share their hard-won successes and dieting challenges.

At the other extreme, I've done research on morbidly obese people who used bariatric surgery—"stomach stapling"—as a means of weight loss. This is definitely a radical approach to losing weight, one that carries the same health risks as any major surgery—including infection and death.

A California-based company called Comprehensive Weight Management asked me to write a psychological behavior-modification program for their patients who'd had bariatric surgery. At first, I was very, very skeptical of this procedure, primarily because ten years ago I knew of someone who died shortly after his stomach-stapling surgery.

But my research revealed two things that surprised me: One is that the operation has changed radically in the last ten years, and is even touted by the National Institutes of Health as a "viable option" for treating morbid (100 pounds overweight or more) obesity. In other words, the operation's safety record is very high now. Many doctors argue that when someone carries 100 extra pounds on the body, the risks of obesity outweigh the risks of the operation.

But more important to me were the personal experiences that were recounted to me by the women who'd undergone the operation. These women were so grateful that they'd been able to have this surgery. Over and over again, I heard stories from women who had been so obese that they were practically bedridden. They couldn't work, play with their kids, or have sex with their husbands. In other words, they didn't have much of a life. And the prospect of trying out another traditional diet didn't appeal to them, as it could have taken three years to drop all the excess weight.

The surgery was their way of making a forced choice. Following the surgery, these women had no choice but to eat extremely small portions of food. Also, both before and after the surgery, these women underwent intensive psychotherapy, which allowed years of pent-up emotions and memories to flood to the surface. A staff psychologist and my behavior-modification program were there to guide and support them as well.

Yes, my feelings about bariatric surgery definitely changed after spending time with these post-operative patients. Many times I heard these women say, "I would have died from the fat without this surgery. I needed to be forced to give up food so I could get in touch with the feelings that made me eat so much."

Indeed, anyone who becomes 100, 200, or more pounds overweight has little prospects for a normal life without radical intervention. I would hope that bariatric surgery is viewed as a last- ditch attempt after every other method is tried and exhausted. No surgery should be viewed as a cure-all. After all, these stomach-stapling patients have to abstain from their old eating habits or risk rupturing their stapling lines. And the only way they can abstain from overeating is by turning to the intensive psychotherapy I've described.

Remember, there's nothing wrong with asking for help. If you're like most overeaters I've worked with, you're a very competent, bright person who usually has a lot of control over her life. It's frustrating to know that there's one area of your life that is out of control—especially when you know what to do to address it! That's why relying on different methods of support, such as a self-help book like this one, a therapist, or a support group, can give you that extra impetus we all need from time to time.

Keep going. You're doing a great job to have read this far, and there's so much more to learn. Don't forget: *You're worth all the effort.*

chapter thirteen

LISTENING TO FOOD CRAVINGS

"I was angry with my friend:
I told my wrath, my wrath did end.
I was angry with my foe:
I told it not, my wrath did grow."
— William Blake

If you eat one piece or serving of something—a candy bar; slice of cake, a hamburger, or whatever—it doesn't necessarily mean you're trying to regulate your mood and energy levels. But if you feel compelled to consume large portions of a certain type of food *all of a sudden,* you're probably eating to anesthetize troubling emotions. That is, you're experiencing tension, depression, anxiety, or boredom (which is really loneliness combined with frustration that life is too routine) and you want to feel better fast.

The chemicals, ingredients, textures, tastes, and smells in most foods directly affect emotions and energy levels. After studying the individual effects of many of the mood/energy-regulating properties of certain foods, I've concluded that there is a very definite correlation between food cravings and emotional issues.

Here's an example of the cyclical nature of this interrelationship: Betty feels depressed, so she reaches for a food that she knows intuitively from past experience will ease her depression—chocolate ice cream. It makes her feel better because of its natural antidepressant properties, texture, and, of course, taste. However, she consumes so much ice cream that she feels even more depressed later. This depression, stemming from her weight problem and other challenges in her life, compels her to eat even more chocolate ice cream the next day. And the cycle goes on and on, sometimes for a lifetime.

Without going into a complex chemistry lecture, let me briefly explain how a food such as chocolate ice cream functions as an antidepressant. When you look at the combination of effects from the ingredients in this dessert, you will see that they trigger a reaction in people that is very similar to that resulting from the ingestion of prescription antidepressant drugs.

First, take a look at a breakdown of some of the properties in chocolate ice cream:

Ingredient/Characteristic	*Effect on Mood/Energy*
1. Choline	Soothing
2. L-Tryptophane mixed with carbohydrate	Calming
3. Phenylethylamine (PEA; the "love drug")	Feeling loved
4. Theobromine	Temporarily energizing
5. Tyramine	Temporarily energizing
6. Caffeine	Temporarily energizing
7. Magnesium	Relaxing

8. Pyrazine	Pleasure-inducing
9. Fat	Calming and filling
10. Sugar	Temporarily energizing
11. Creamy texture	Comforting

And this is just a partial list! It does show, however, that chocolate ice cream both soothes and comforts you while, at the same time, also reenergizing you temporarily. In other words, after eating chocolate ice cream, you feel renewed and ready to go—similar to the way you would feel if you were taking prescription antidepressant drugs. As far as I'm concerned, chocolate ice cream is an incredibly powerful antidepressant "drug," and it's over-the-counter!

Chocolate frozen yogurt produces a similar effect, but because it may lack fat or sugar, yogurt won't sedate you as effectively as ice cream does. Also, carob, which is often used instead of chocolate in "health" foods, doesn't have the same chemical properties as chocolate, so carob yogurt or ice cream is in another category altogether.

Most of the other foods that people commonly overeat have similar food-mood correlations. Through my treatment of, and discussion with, clients all across the country, I've found that the connection between food, mood, and emotions depicted on the chart that follows almost always exists.

People in all walks of life have asked me what their food cravings say about their personality. I base my answer on the material I've compiled in the following chart. And these people almost always exclaim in response, "You're absolutely right! That's exactly how I am."

I really went out on a limb when I was with Phil Donahue, Geraldo Rivera, and Sally Jessy Raphael while appearing on their respective shows at different times. I asked all three hosts to tell me which foods they crave or binge on. Interestingly, Donahue, Geraldo, and Sally Jessy all crave salty, spicy foods. On national television, I unhesitantly told each of them that people who crave or overeat salty, spicy foods usually also crave stimulation and excitement. All three talk show hosts confirmed that what I said was true.

People who eat these types of foods tend to take huge risks in life. They face challenges head-on, and if they fail, they try again. This is true for Donahue, Geraldo, and Sally Jessy. They all crave salty, spicy foods; and they all relish excitement and stimulation. That's how they withstand the pressures of being in the limelight, dealing with rating wars, and the like.

What follows is a list of commonly overeaten foods, together with the emotions that usually precipitate a craving for them. Each item on the list contains chemicals, textures, and smells that break down in much the same manner as chocolate ice cream does. (You'll find an extensive list of hundreds of foods that we crave, their underlying meanings, healing affirmations for each food craving, and also scientific research explaining the food-mood links, in my book *Constant Craving: What Your Food Cravings Mean and How to Overcome Them* (Hay House, 1995). Or, you can purchase just the food craving and meaning chart, without the scientific explanations, in my book *Constant Craving A–Z* (also by Hay House, 1999).

The only exception to the information provided on this chart is if an extremely positive or negative emotion is associated with a certain food. For example, if Grandma always served you chicken soup when you were sick, you may feel nauseated every time you smell chicken broth—regardless of the chemical properties in the soup. Or, if Mom always fixed you a special snack of cookies and milk after school, you may associate that snack with feelings of love and warmth.

In general, though, I've found that my research findings on food and mood, as outlined below, to be incredibly accurate. This chart will not only help you understand what is behind your food cravings, but will also give you the wherewithal to address these underlying emotions instead of covering them up with food.

Food	*Associated Emotional/ Personality Traits*
1. Chocolate candy bars, plain	You desire stimulation, or feel deprived of love
2. Crunchy chocolate candy, including chocolate bars with nuts	You feel frustrated, anxious, or angry because of tension or lack of love.
3. Chocolate ice cream	You feel depressed, usually due to tension, or difficulty in a relationship.
4. Chocolate chip, rocky road, or any crunchy chocolate ice cream	You're holding anger in, or feel angry at yourself, resulting in depression.
5. Mint chocolate chip ice cream	You feel lethargic and frustrated because you've got more responsibilities than time or motivation.
6. Chocolate pudding	You desire comfort, nurturing, and hugs.
7. Chocolate cake	You feel empty, insecure, possibly from a lack of love.

8. Hot chocolate

You've saved up hurt feelings throughout the day, and now want to ease your ego so you can sleep.

9. Crunchy, high-fat foods (fried chicken, chips, fries, etc.)

You feel empty because of frustration or anger.

10. Spicy foods topped with dairy products (pizza with extra cheese; Mexican food with cheese and sour cream)

You feel depressed because life seems dull.

11. Dairy products (cheese, yogurt, etc.)

You feel depressed or unloved; you desire nurturing and comfort.

12. Baked goods, pastries

You feel tense and really need to relax. You may also feel that your life is empty.

13. Crunchy foods topped with dairy products (crackers and cheese; chips and dip; nachos with cheese and no salsa; salad with blue cheese dressing, etc.)

You're holding in anger, resentment, and/or frustration, resulting in depression.

14. Sugary sweets

You want to feel energetic, or to overcome burnout.

| 15. | Colas, diet or regular | You feel overwhelmed by work or chores; you want to have more energy; you'd also like to feel more sexual energy. |
| 16. | Hamburgers and other high-fat fast foods | You feel empty or dissatisfied with some aspects of life. You may also feel insecure or inadequate in some area of life. |

By understanding the food-mood connections, you'll be in a better position to control your compulsive binge eating. The best method to use is in this regard may also sound too easy to you. However, the feedback that I receive from my thousands of clients and workshop attendees is that: *It works!*

Here it is: The next time you suddenly feel very hungry—meaning, out-of-the-blue hungry—promise me that you won't go near any food for 15 minutes. Get out of the house if you have to. If you're at work, go into the ladies' room or some other area where there's no food. Throw any tempting food items down the garbage disposal if you can't leave your home or room (don't put the food in the trash, because sometimes desperate people dig it back out again). Bottom line: No matter what you have to do, don't eat anything for 15 minutes after first feeling hunger pangs.

Then, ask yourself: "Could I possibly be feeling an emotion that I'm uncomfortable with? Am I feeling drained or tense? Am I trying to use food as a pick-me-up?" Most people find that by using this two-step method, they're able to control their food cravings to a greater extent, thus exercising more control over their appetite and actions.

Physically Based Cravings

Not all food cravings are triggered by emotions. There are very real physical reasons why you crave certain foods, usually due to vitamin or mineral deficiencies.

When the body lacks certain essential minerals, vitamins, and amino acids, food cravings act as a signal, similar to a low-fuel warning light on a car dashboard. There are often deficiencies with respect to minerals such as magnesium, chromium, calcium, the B vitamins, vitamin C, and amino acids such as tryptophan. (Children with hyperactivity are often found to be deficient in magnesium.)

Tryptophan—commonly found in proteins such as dairy and red meat products—is a catalyst for creating the brain chemical serotonin. As mentioned earlier, serotonin plays a major role in determining your mood, energy level and the quality of your sleep. When serotonin becomes depleted, the body signals include carbohydrate cravings, mood swings, irritability, fatigue, a decreased desire for sex, and insomnia.

Magnesium, chromium, and calcium are also crucial to your physical and mental health. When your body lacks any of these minerals, your energy level drops. You may feel somewhat depressed without really knowing why. You crave food—not only to replenish these minerals, but also due to your desire to draw energy from the natural stimulants in food.

B vitamins also play an important role in energy regulation. Unfortunately, whenever we eat "junk food" or anything that contains "empty" calories, we deplete our body's B vitamins because it takes B vitamins to digest any substance we ingest. If we eat potato chips, for example, we'll use B vitamins to digest them. Since the potato chips don't contain any B vitamins, we will have used B vitamins without replacing them. We'll be in a B-vitamin deficit, and this will trigger food cravings.

When C vitamins are at a low level in the body, we may crave salad, tomatoes, or other fruits and vegetables. Unfortunately, many compulsive overeaters turn to high-fat versions of salads and vegetable dishes to fulfill these otherwise-healthful cravings.

Vitamin, mineral, and amino acid depletions occur because of tension, environmental or dietary pollutants, too stringent dieting, alcohol or drug abuse (including caffeine abuse), insomnia, or the onset of the menstrual cycle. The eating plan in this book circumvents food cravings by providing a menu high in vitamins, minerals, and amino acids.

I think it's important to eat a very healthy diet in order to feel and look your best. What's the point of *looking* slim and trim if you can't enjoy it because you don't *feel* good? I'm also a great believer in taking vitamin and mineral supplements. Vitamins B-6 and B-12; and the minerals magnesium, chromium picolinate, and calcium, all help combat food cravings. If your body has adequate amounts of these substances, you'll be less apt to overeat.

chapter fourteen

EATING IN SECRET, EATING IN SHAME

"He that respects himself is safe from others;
He wears a coat of mail that none can pierce."
— Henry Wadsworth Longfellow

Brenda's Story

Every evening after dinner, Brenda patiently waited until her family went to bed. She always managed to come up with a good excuse for why she wanted to stay up. "I want to finish this chapter in the book I'm reading," she'd tell her husband, or *The Tonight Show* is having that comedian on who I like so much."

She wouldn't dare admit her true motivation for staying awake while the others slept—to be alone with her favorite dessert of ice cream and cake. About a half hour after her husband had gone to bed, when Brenda was sure she couldn't hear him rustling in the bedroom anymore, she'd make her move.

Quietly, in fact, so softly that no one could possibly hear her, Brenda would slip into the kitchen. And then, as carefully as she could, she'd open the freezer door and pull out the carton of ice cream. She'd hold her breath while lifting the carton's lid so that the sound of the air suction and cardboard rubbing against one another wouldn't awaken anyone.

Sometimes, Brenda would think that she heard someone coming, so she'd quickly shove the ice cream into a cupboard. But when she was sure she was alone and had successfully retrieved her ice cream and cake without a sound, Brenda would stand in the laundry room where no one could see her.

Being alone with her desserts was sheer bliss to Brenda. She was by herself, where no one could criticize her for going off her diet or make her think about what she was really doing.

In truth, though, people like Brenda aren't alone in their behavior. There are thousands, perhaps millions, of "Closet Bingers" —people who feel the need to sneak and hide when eating their favorite food. Some conceal candy bars in the bottom of their purse; some keep cupcakes hidden in the glove compartment; some stoop down behind open refrigerator doors so that others won't see them eating with utter abandonment. And I've had clients tell me they kept food hidden in the bathroom, where they could eat in complete privacy.

But the person the Closet Binger most wants to hide from is . . . herself.

Closet Bingeing and Self-Esteem

I've talked to and treated hundreds of Closet Bingers who were single and living alone. And yet, even though they weren't sharing their living space with anyone, they were still afraid that someone else might "catch" them eating something fattening.

— My client Sue comes to mind when I think of someone who would sneak-eat, even though there was no one in her life to hide the eating from. During her first therapy session, Sue blurted out that the only way she was going to be able to recover from compulsive overeating was to remove her large stash of candy bars from her car. I walked out to the parking lot to help her, and together we filled up my medium-sized office trash can with boxes of Hershey's bars, Nestle's Crunch bars, and dozens of crumpled old candy wrappers.

With Closet Bingers such as Sue, the compulsive nature of eating isn't just the appeal of the food. Instead, the rush of sneaking around—the aura of "badness" and "naughtiness"—is a huge part of the appeal. Most people have relished the joy of being naughty in a harmless sort of way. And even though there is that heart-pounding fear involved in possibly being caught in the act, there is also a form of excitement inherent in the process. So the Closet Binger who successfully pulls off a binge may actually congratulate herself for getting away with an ingeniously master-minded plan.

Closet Bingeing is also a silent form of rebellion against real or perceived pressures to be a "good girl," pressures that usually start in childhood.

— Sue learned early in life that attention and praise were heaped upon her when she acted "sweet" and when she got A's on her report card. Her parents constantly referred to her as "our problem-free child." So how could Sue ever let her parents down? She couldn't. Sue found that complying to others' wishes was the fastest route to gaining approval—a habit that followed her into adulthood.

However, it's normal for overly compliant people to rebel from time to time. No one can maintain a false persona of being in a cheerful, understanding mood all the time. In my practice, I've found that many "good girls" silently try to regain control over their lives by gorging on food when others aren't looking.

Many times, these women grew up in households where a lot of attention was paid to their physical appearance and weight. Messages such as, "Better cut down on the calories because your rear end is starting to get big," are common in Closet Binger households. In other words, part of being a "good girl" implicitly means watching out for fattening foods and calories. Sadly, the young Closet Binger is usually unaware of the fact that it is *her* body, and therefore her right, to regulate whatever foods she eats, as well as the type of figure she chooses to maintain.

Sneak-eating usually starts in childhood. This is not a simple case of children stealing cookies from the cookie jar, although that *can* be one symptom of early childhood Closet Binging. Instead, sneak-eating is a process where the person feels unsafe indulging in pleasurable obsessive eating around others. There's an underlying fear that if she's caught eating something "bad" (ice cream, cake, candy, etc.), then the "privilege" of eating this food will be suspended. And, on top of that, she'll be punished by having the other person see her as less than perfect.

To the Closet Binger, it's easier to hide her imperfect behavior—such as obsessive eating—from the rest of the world, and to present the face of a competent superwoman or supergirl for everyone else to see. But she also denies to herself that she's sneak-eating. In other words, she's not only hiding from others, but from herself, too.

What's particularly interesting to me is that sneak-eaters are often extremely accomplished women. Every aspect of their lives—career, relationships, finances—appears to be under control. But, for the sneak-eater, a very crucial part of her life—revolving around eating and weight gain—is completely out of control.

Breaking the Eat-and-Sneak Cycle

Closet Bingers who examine their motivations for sneak-eating are far less apt to continue closet overeating than people who never examine their motivations.

> — My client Samantha, for example, said that I was the first person she'd ever admitted her sneak-eating habits to. Just by opening up about her secretive eating, Samantha found that she wasn't comfortable the next time she began to sneak-eat. After being honest with me, it was difficult to hide what she was really doing from herself.

I believe that self-honesty is a key factor in breaking any addictive cycle because so much of compulsive eating, drinking, shopping, and so on, is really just a way to avoid looking inside oneself. In other words, many people engage in addictions because they're running away from something inside themselves or something in their lives that they don't want to examine.

I've dealt with many Closet Binger clients who were sneak-eating to avoid looking at their unhappy marriages or jobs. Other clients were afraid to acknowledge how much anger they were carrying around inside. And still others were struggling with insecurities—"Am I an okay person?"—and mistakenly were assuming that if they admitted this fear to themselves, then it would undoubtedly become a reality.

Abuse survivors, guarded and mistrusting of others, often sneak-eat because it doesn't feel safe to openly engage in the very private affair called eating. Others sneak-eat to avoid ridicule or scorn.

Eating in private isn't unhealthful in and of itself. The problem is that the act of sneak-eating fuels massive and obsessive consumption of food. When you fear being caught, or you feel you're doing something wrong or "naughty," your anxiety level elevates. This anxiety then triggers an eating binge. So, for all intents and purposes, you overeat to calm the nervousness triggered by overeating in the first place! Ironic, isn't it? Yet, there *are* steps you can take when the sneak-eating urge crops up:

1. Remember that no matter whom you hide from, or how much you deny to yourself what you're doing, the calories from your binge will show up on *your* body. In the end, it probably doesn't matter to anyone else, as much as it does to you, how much you weigh or how you feel inside your body.

2. Also try to consider this: Sneak-eating really isn't as much fun as you may believe. If you're really honest with yourself, I think you'll agree that sneak-eating makes you feel bad about yourself.

3. Start keeping a food diary, and write down every single thing you eat and drink. The diary doesn't have to be anything fancy—just a little notepad you get at the drugstore. Even if you're ashamed of something you ate, write it down anyway. This will not only get you in the habit of honestly coming to terms with what you're eating, it will also remind you to keep your portions small and your food content low.

Once you honestly confront the Closet Bingeing issue, it becomes fairly easy to break out of it. I've seen many people achieve great success by employing the methods described in this chapter. And the good news is that after putting this habit behind them, it's usually gone for good!

chapter fifteen

LIQUIDS:
THIRST, WATER, AND ALCOHOL

*"It is necessary to the happiness of a man that
he be mentally faithful to himself."*
— Thomas Paine

The liquids you drink can be just as important to your diet as the foods you eat when you're trying to maintain your weight. Many dieters—particularly "chocoholics" who tend to abuse psychoactive (mood-altering) chemicals in ordinary foods—drink too much diet cola.

The reason I say "too much" is because diet or regular cola, if consumed in too great a quantity, makes dieting a difficult process and even slows weight loss. There are three main problems associated with drinking diet colas while trying to lose weight:

1. A 12-ounce can of diet cola contains roughly 70 milligrams of sodium. This may not seem high when you consider that the recommended sodium consumption for a dieting woman is 1,000 milligrams a day. However, consider this: If you drink four sodas

a day, that's 280 milligrams of sodium! And when you add that sodium to all the salt you normally consume in food, you can easily exceed the 1,000-milligram-per-day level.

Besides being linked to high blood pressure, the foremost concern about sodium for dieters is that it causes water retention. Dieters struggling with weight plateaus often have to cut their diet cola consumption down to a maximum of two cans a day before weight loss can continue.

2. Colas contain about as much caffeine as a half-cup of coffee. The caffeine in colas is made from kola nut extract, and regulations keep the caffeine content at a maximum of 0.02 percent of the soda.

However, when dieters drink a great deal of soda (more than two cans a day), the caffeine amount accumulates; and nervous, excited, jittery, or anxious feelings can result. Also, one of the amino acids in the sweetener aspartame (NutraSweet brand sweetener) called "phenylalanine," acts as a natural stimulant, which makes some individuals feel dizzy, lightheaded, or anxious. The resulting Tension, from caffeine and phenylalanine, can trigger a desire to overeat, as the dieter seeks to calm down through the use of food.

3. Cola can reduce your magnesium levels, thereby triggering food cravings. A study conducted at East Tennessee State University found that phosphoric acid in cola binds with magnesium in the body, and extracts the latter. Each 12-ounce can of cola

contains 36 milligrams of phosphoric acid, and the result is that 36 milligrams of magnesium are removed from the body.

In light of the information above, you can probably see why it's important to cut down or eliminate your consumption of soda. However, if you feel you can't live without diet cola, then limit your intake to two cans or 24 ounces a day.

A Half-Gallon A Day . . .

The ideal drink, as you may already know, is water. I recommend drinking at least a half-gallon a day. This can sound like a lot, to be sure. What really works for me is to get in the habit of keeping one-gallon bottles of spring water around at all times to serve as a reminder to drink water. Buy several bottles at the store (they're not that expensive, especially compared to the price of cola), and carry one to work with you each day.

Water is beneficial to dieters for several reasons:

- It makes you feel full, so you won't be as hungry.

- It is actually more energizing than a cup of coffee, so you won't be as apt to reach for a sugary food to try and pep yourself up.

- It flushes salt out of the body, thereby reducing water retention.

I've found that the feeling of being deprived because you're drinking "plain old boring water" is negated by turning the water into a special drink. Two easy ways to accomplish this are to pour the water into a special glass, and to garnish it with a slice of lemon or lime.

A Word about Alcohol

Perhaps the most striking observation I've made in working with compulsive overeaters is the high incidence (over 95 percent) of alcoholism in their extended family. Almost all of my clients had either parents or grandparents who drank alcohol in a dependent or abusive manner. Even my clients who initially denied that alcoholism ran in their family usually found, after asking other family members that, yes, Grandpa was in fact an alcoholic. Of course, nobody in the family ever talked about it. Instead, they said that Grandpa died of cirrhosis of the liver, a heart attack, or some other alcoholism-related disease.

The purpose of this discussion is not to point the finger of blame, as in "It's Grandpa's fault" that you compulsively overeat. But it is important to understand the role that alcoholism may have played, or is playing, in your life.

The majority of studies on alcoholism in families overwhelmingly points to a genetic link that causes an alcoholic predisposition—that is, *there is a greater propensity toward alcoholism than in people from nonalcoholic families.* Although only about 10 percent of people in the general population develop problems with alcoholism, having one alcoholic parent increases your chances of developing alcoholism by more than 30 percent. And if your mother and father were *both* alcoholic, your risk is greater than 50 percent!

Sugar Addiction and Alcoholism

Alcohol and sugar are almost identical in molecular structure. Therefore, people prone to alcoholism have a reaction to sugar that mimics the alcoholic reaction to alcohol. This reaction manifests itself as a combination of changes in the brain's chemistry and electrical activity, and a craving for more alcohol or sugar.

The alcoholic body has a difficult time distinguishing between alcohol and sugar, and feels the need to binge on one or both substances, which makes sense when you consider that alcohol is created out of food: Wine is fermented fruit; beer is made from grain; vodka from potatoes; and so on.

I've also found that female children and grandchildren of alcoholics are more apt to choose refined sugar over alcohol as their "feel-good drug" of choice. I believe this occurs for two reasons:

1. Social pressures train young females to be "good little girls," motivating females to pick "the good little girl's drug": sugar.

2. Most likely, the girl's mother was herself a compulsive eater and sugar binger. The little girl watched her mother overeat sugar and use sugar as a tension-management tool, and this reinforced the girl's likelihood of abusing sugar later on in life.

Those Abused by Alcohol Often Grow Up to Do the Same

Professionals such as myself, who have specialized in treating addictions, bear witness to a common family scenario: Compulsive overeaters and alcoholics are often married to each other. In many of my clients' families, we charted "family trees" of addictions running through the generations. The most prevalent pattern I saw was that males abused alcohol; and their wives, sisters and daughters had eating disorders.

A lot of this stemmed from societal pressures for females to be "good girls," as stated previously. Women are more apt to choose a socially sanctioned substance—food—to make themselves feel better. Men are more easily "forgiven," if you will, for sitting around and having a few drinks.

The result is that women who do abuse alcohol often do so in private. As is the case with Closet Bingers who sneak-eat when no one's looking, Closet Drinkers gulp their wine, beer, and vodka in private. They don't want anyone to know they're drinking, and out of shame, they abuse alcohol when they're alone.

Those suffering from the pound/pain link are especially prone to alcohol abuse. Sexual, physical, and emotional abuse survivors often come from alcoholic households. Fathers who molest their daughters are usually drunk at the time, and the mother may be passed out on the sofa from an afternoon of drinking. The little girl grows up watching her parents turn to alcohol to relax, or manage tension. As an abuse survivor, she grows up feeling tense herself—since she hasn't learned how to relax and trust people—so she turns to alcohol, just as her parents "taught" her.

Researchers in the late '80s studied 48 adolescents who had been sexually abused and found that they were much more likely to abuse alcohol and other drugs than adolescents who had not been sexually abused. Other studies (Benward, 1975; Cohen, 1982; Rohsenow, 1988) have found that between 30 and 44 percent of people diagnosed as addicted to drugs or alcohol have a history of sexual abuse. This is a much higher percentage than is found in the general population of nonsubstance abusers.

Studies of brain chemistry in alcoholics point to physical reasons behind alcoholism. We know there are genetic predispositions for alcoholism; in other words, you can *inherit* the desire to abuse alcohol. Several researchers have discovered that the brain chemical serotonin may be depleted in alcoholic brains. As you may recall from previous chapters, when serotonin is low, you feel lethargic or irritable. Researchers believe that alcoholics may be self-medicating, attempting to atone for the depleted serotonin by getting drunk.

Unfortunately, alcohol abuse results in further serotonin depletion. Serotonin is a chemical that forms in the brain while you sleep. Your brain doesn't store the substance; it must be created from scratch every night. What happens is this: Your body converts a body substance, melatonin, into the brain chemical serotonin during the Rapid Eye Movement (REM) phase of the nightly sleep cycle. If your REM sleep cycle is interrupted, you won't create enough serotonin. And then you'll wake up feeling groggy.

Excessive consumption of alcohol and other drugs interferes with REM sleep. If you drink too much before bed, you won't get enough REM sleep and you'll wake up with a hangover from depleted serotonin. Those suffering from the pound/pain link may notice that they crave carbohydrates (breads, sweets, starchy foods) when their serotonin is low.

Even worse: Alcohol interferes with weight-loss programs.

First, alcohol is very fattening. Just look at how many calories are in a typical drink, keeping in mind that most people have more than one drink at a sitting:

Alcoholic Beverage	Calories Consumed
Beer, 12 oz.	150
Brandy, 1 oz.	75
Champagne, dry, 4 oz.	105
Champagne, sweet, 4 oz.	160
Daiquiri, 3½ oz.	125
Distilled liquors	100
(gin, rum, vodka, whiskey, 80 proof, 1½ oz.)	
Martini, 3½ oz.	140
Tom Collins, 10 oz.	180
Wine, red, 3½ oz.	85
Wine, white, 3½ oz.	80

Second, alcohol slows the body down. It is a depressant. But, whoops! It especially slows down metabolism, the rate at which your body burns calories. So, not only does alcohol *add* calories to your body, but it also makes you burn those calories at a slower rate.

Third, wine and beer contain sulfites, which cause edema (or water retention) and other allergic reactions in many people. This naturally occurring substance is in all wines and beers, including organic varieties. Non-organic wines contain even larger amounts of sulfites, as this substance is added as a preservative. That's why your face or other body parts may appear swollen after a night of heavy wine or beer consumption.

Finally—and you're probably aware of this from personal experience—if you've been drinking or you're hungover, you're less likely to exercise. Even though a workout would probably make you feel much better, when you're tired or irritated, you just want to relax. So, you burn even fewer calories because you're less active.

There's nothing wrong with drinking alcohol in moderation (as long as you don't drive after doing so). It's just important to drink wisely and choose low-calorie alcoholic drinks such as dry white wine mixed with sparkling soda. Of course, people with a predisposition toward alcoholism, as well as those who are confirmed alcoholics, are well advised to abstain completely from alcohol.

The support group, Alcoholics Anonymous (who could assist you in getting a sponsor if you desire one), in conjunction with psychotherapeutic help, can be of enormous assistance to you if you've decided that you wish to give up alcohol.

chapter sixteen

WEIGHING IN—ASKING FOR TROUBLE OR FACING THE TRUTH?

"The greater part of our happiness or misery depends on our dispositions, and not on our circumstances."
— Martha Washington

My peers in the eating disorders field have been known to criticize my position on the concept of weighing oneself. Nonetheless, I stand by my advice, because I so firmly believe in it.

I think it's best to weigh yourself every morning, right after you awaken and urinate. This gives you immediate feedback about your weight and eating habits, which allows you to accurately gauge your weight-loss efforts.

After all, how can you achieve a goal unless you're able to evaluate your progress? How can you abide by the speed limit unless your car has a speedometer to tell you how fast you're going? How can you reach a new destination unless you have a map showing you how to get there?

My peers tend to advise their clients to throw away their scales, because "getting on them every day just places the attention on weight, which will make you hungrier and more focused on food." But while I understand the logic behind this advice,

I don't think it works.

Please let me explain: You see, I'm not advocating extreme reliance on the scale. I don't advise that you weigh yourself more than once a day, and I don't want you to feel that the *quality* of each day is dependent on what the scale says. If your weight is down, it doesn't mean you're a "good" person, any more than having gained a pound means you're a "bad" person.

Weight fluctuations are normal. Salty diets, late-night eating, menstrual cycles—all of these factors can precipitate higher numbers on the scale, without the body actually gaining fat. And some exercise programs actually result in heavier body weights because the increased muscle mass weighs more than the body fat.

I'm advocating the weight scale as a *tool*. Use it in combination with your other tools, such as noticing how you feel (energetic or lethargic, lightheaded, fully able to concentrate?). Do your muscles feel tight and taut, or flabby and soft? Do your clothes feel looser? What is your fat percentage, according to the measuring devices used by health clubs and health-care professionals? The answers to these questions can be combined with the information supplied by the scale.

The intelligent use of a scale is important in maintaining weight loss. Those of us with fluctuating weights are just too prone to lie to ourselves. Without the feedback that the scale provides, it's too easy to return to old, unhealthful eating habits—with the resulting weight gains. In fact, many of my clients reported doing what Bonnie did for years:

— Bonnie had gained and lost 20, 30, or 40 pounds more times than she could remember. Each time she'd lose the weight, she'd feel invincible. "This time, I'll keep it off," she'd swear.

Gradually, however, her strict diets would yield to her normal eating habits. She'd return to using high-fat salad dressings; and would pile nuts, bacon bits, and cheese on her "diet" salads. Bonnie would use extra butter on her bread, and lots of oil in her cooking.

Even though her body was regaining the weight, Bonnie would deny the truth. Her clothes would get tight, but Bonnie would shrug it off, saying, "My clothes must have shrunk." She'd only look at her face in the mirror while getting dressed in the morning. And, of course, she'd avoid weighing herself.

Only months later, when none of her clothes fit, would Bonnie make herself get on the scale. By then, she'd have 30 pounds to lose all over again.

This is why I advocate daily weighing. It provides useful feedback and keeps us from deceiving ourselves (which we're so skilled at doing!). If you use the scale intelligently, it truly is a helpful tool.

Please keep this in mind when using the scale:

• Weight fluctuations are normal. Water retention resulting from high-salt diets and the menstrual cycle can dramatically affect your weight. So, too, can the time of day you weigh yourself. Our body weight can fluctuate by up to eight pounds during the day. That's why weighing yourself first thing in the morning, undressed and after urinating, will give you a truer picture of your weight.

• Keep the scale in a stationary location. Weight readings can fluctuate if you move the scale to different areas of your home.

- Don't weigh yourself more than once a day.

- Please don't measure your self-worth or "what kind of day" you're going to have based on the number on that scale. If you gained weight, then just use the information to take responsible action. Remember, the scale is just a tool that can help you in your weight- loss efforts.

- Your weight doesn't reflect what kind of person you are. It is merely an indicator of how you feel about yourself. As you release your pain and self-blame, the numbers on the scale will bear witness to your "lighter" attitude.

And that feels good!

chapter seventeen

KEEPING THE BODY AND SPIRIT LIGHT

*"Your limits are defined by the agreement
you have made about what is possible. Change that
agreement and you can dissolve all limits."*
— Dr. Wayne W. Dyer, author of
Dr. Wayne Dyer's 10 Secrets for Success and Inner Peace

I've provided you with quite a bit of information in this book, all vital to the long-term success of your weight-loss efforts. Here is a summary of the most important points:

1. Symptoms of unresolved pain include a seemingly out-of-control appetite for food, and body weight that refuses to stay off; in addition to other symptoms such as headaches, back or neck pain, insomnia, depression, cancer, heart problems, and gynecological complaints.

2. To uncover the unresolved pain, you usually need to recall some painful experiences from childhood and/or adolescence and determine

who the perpetrator was. If you blamed yourself for any abuse that you suffered, then you need to remind yourself that, as a young person, you weren't responsible for the abusive or neglectful actions of others—even if you somehow felt responsible at the time.

3. Your overactive appetite is actually triggered by one of these emotions: Fear, Anger, Tension, and Shame (FATS). When you feel hungry, you must avoid automatic eating and ask yourself if one of these four feelings is triggering the hunger.

4. You can use exercise, affirmations, and visualization techniques to transform the FATS feelings into Forgiving, Accepting, and Trusting your Self. An overactive appetite is a signal that you're not happy, probably because you're not fulfilling your Divine mission or true purpose in life. You can effectively use your new tools to begin working toward your dream life.

5. As you feel more safe, secure, and confident, your appetite will naturally diminish. You will no longer need the shield that fat gave you, and you won't need to mask your pain with food any longer. Your weight will drop, since your body is meant to be normal in size.

6. You can release the pain, and you no longer have to hold on to self-loathing. You know that it's important

to love yourself and the little girl inside you. You can turn your FATS feelings into a big "Forget All That Stuff" and leave the painful memories behind you. Memories serve a purpose—they help you realize why you were mad at yourself. But once you've done so, and have released your self-blame, you can forget about the past. You're not broken or damaged—you're whole and complete because God made you in His image and likeness.

You Deserve a Light Life!

Right this minute, you're deciding on the size and health of your body. If you're reading this paragraph while exercising, drinking water, eating low-fat foods, or snacking on fruit, the sum total of your nutritional and exercise habits will show up on your scale every day. If you don't weigh yourself, the sum total is evident in other ways: your energy level, mood, and the way your clothes feel on your body.

Remember, I'm not asking you to deprive yourself in any way or to embark on a stringent diet. What I am suggesting is that you approach the issues connected to health and weight from a positive standpoint.

That is, discard the type of negative thinking that says: "I have to avoid bad foods," "I can't eat sweets or junk food," "I have to lose weight; I'm so fat," and replace these thoughts with positive affirmations, such as: "It feels good to eat fresh, healthful foods," "I have so much energy when I eat fruit, vegetables, and whole grains," and "I'm choosing to live in a healthy, fit body."

And, please, let me leave you with one other important piece of information to "digest": No matter how good a piece of food tastes, the taste is fleeting and the fat is lasting. What certain dieting organizations profess in their meetings is absolutely true: "Nothing tastes as good as thin feels." Food is a quick fix for troubling emotions and thoughts, but the results last about as long as a small bandage on a severed artery.

Listen to your food cravings—they are a part of your inner voice and provide valuable information. Listen to your feelings— the more powerful and troubling they are, the more urgent their message is to you. Listen to your inner vision, where you will "see" the life of your dreams—this is the road map that will enable you to fulfill your life's mission. And when you fulfill your purpose, you also fill up any emptiness and insecurity. You'll no longer require excess food at that point.

My sincere wish is that you treat your body and soul with compassion and kindness. Love that little child inside of you, and be understanding when she occasionally falters. Give her lots of hugs and encouragement, and she'll reward you with lots and lots of smiles from deep inside of you—smiles that are more delicious than any food you could possibly eat.

I wish the very best for you! And please know that I will be with you in spirit every step of the way!

Self-Help Resources

The following list of resources can be used to access information on a variety of issues. The addresses and telephone numbers listed are for the national headquarters; look in your local Yellow Pages under "Community Services" for resources closer to your area.

In addition to the following groups, other self-help organizations may be available in your area to assist your healing and recovery for a particular life crisis not listed here. Consult your telephone directory, call a counseling center or help line near you, or contact:

AIDS

CBC National AIDS Hotline
(800) 342-2437

Children with AIDS (CWA)
Project of America
(800) 866-AIDS
(24-hour hotline)

The Names Project—
AIDS Quilt
(800) 872-6263

Project Inform
19655 Market St., Ste. 220
San Francisco, CA 94103
(415) 558-8669

PWA Coalition
50 W. 17th St.
New York, NY 10011

Spanish HIV/STD/AIDS
Hotline
(800) 344-7432

TTY (Hearing Impaired)
AIDS Hotline
(CDC National HIV/AIDS)
(800) 243-7889

ALCOHOL ABUSE

Al-Anon Family Headquarters
1600 Corporate Landing Parkway
Virginia Beach, VA 23454-5617
(800) 4AL-ANON

Alcoholics Anonymous (AA)
General Service Office
475 Riverside Dr.
New York, NY 10115
(212) 870-3400

Children of Alcoholics Foundation
164 W. 74th St.
New York, NY 10023
(800) 359-COAF

Mothers Against Drunk Driving (MADD)
(254) 690-6233

National Association of Children of Alcoholics (NACOA)
11426 Rockville Pike, Ste. 100
Rockville, MD 20852
(301) 468-0985
(888) 554-2627

National Clearinghouse for Alcohol and Drug Information (NCADI)
P.O. Box 234
Rockville, MD 20852
(301) 468-2600

National Council on Alcoholism and Drug Dependence (NCADD)
12 West 21st St.
New York, NY 10010
(212) 206-6770
(800) 475-HOPE

Women for Sobriety
(800) 333-1606

ALZHEIMER'S DISEASE

Alzheimer's Association
919 N. Michigan Ave., Ste. 1100
Chicago, IL 60611
(800) 621-0379
www.alz.org

Alzheimer's Disease Education and Referral Center
P.O. Box 8250
Silver Spring, MD 20907
(800) 438-4380
adear@alzheimers.org

Eldercare Locator
927 15th St. NW, 6th Fl.
Washington, DC 20005
(800) 677-1116

CANCER

National Cancer Institute
(800) 4-CANCER

CHILDREN'S ISSUES

Child Molestation

**Child Help USA/
Child Abuse Hotline**
232 East Gish Rd.
San Jose, CA 95112
(800) 422-4453

Prevent Child Abuse America
200 South Michigan Ave., Ste. 17
Chicago, IL 60604
(312) 663-3520

Crisis Intervention

Boy's Town National Hotline
(800) 448-3000

Children of the Night
P.O. Box 4343
Hollywood, CA 90078
(800) 551-1300

Covenant House Hotline
(800) 999-9999

Kid Save Line
(800) 543-7283

Youth Nineline
(referrals for parents/teens about drugs, homelessness, runaways)
(800) 999-9999

Missing Children
**Missing Children . . .
HELP Center**
410 Ware Blvd., Ste. 710
Tampa, FL 33619
(800) USA-KIDS

National Center for Missing and Exploited Children
699 Prince St.
Alexandria, VA 22314
(800) 843-5678

Children with Serious Illnesses
(fulfilling wishes):

Brass Ring Society
National Headquarters
213 N. Washington St.
Snow Hill, MD 21863
(410) 632-4700
(800) 666-WISH

Make-a-Wish Foundation
(800) 332-9474

CO-DEPENDENCY

Co-Dependents Anonymous
(602) 277-7991

DEATH/GRIEVING/SUICIDE

Grief Recovery Institute
P.O. Box 461659
Los Angeles, CA 90046-1659
(323) 650-1234
www/grief-recovery.com

National Hospice and Palliative Care Organization
1700 Diagonal Rd., Ste. 300
Alexandria, VA 22314
(703) 243-5900
www.nhpco.org

SIDS (Sudden Infant Death Syndrome) Alliance
1314 Bedford Ave., Ste. 210
Baltimore, MD 21208

Parents of Murdered Children
(recovering from violent death of friend or family member)
100 E 8th St., Ste. B41
Cincinnati, OH 45202
(513) 721-5683

Survivors of Suicide
Call your local Mental Health Association for the branch nearest you.

AARP Grief and Loss Programs
(202) 434-2260
(800) 424-3410 ext. 2260

DEBTS

Credit Referral
(information on local credit counseling services)
(800) 388-CCCS

Debtors Anonymous
General Service Board
P.O. Box 888
Needham, MA 02492-0009
(781) 453-2743
www.debtorsanonymous.org

DIABETES

American Diabetes Association
(800) 232-3472

DOMESTIC VIOLENCE

National Coalition Against Domestic Violence
P.O. Box 34103
Washington, DC 20043-4103
(202) 745-1211

**National Domestic Violence
Hotline**
P.O. Box 161810
Austin, TX 78716
(800) 799-SAFE
DRUG ABUSE

**Cocaine Anonymous National
Referral Line**
(800) 347-8998

**National Helpline of
Phoenix House**
(cocaine abuse hotline)
(800) 262-2463
(800) COCAINE
www.drughelp.org

**National Institute of Drug
Abuse (NIDA)**
6001 Executive Blvd., Rm. 5213
Bethesda, MD 20892-9561
Parklawn Building
(301) 443-6245 (for information)
(800) 662-4357 (for help)

World Service Office, Inc. (CA)
3740 Overland Ave., Ste. C
Los Angeles, CA 90034-6337
(310) 559-5833
(800) 347-8998 (to leave
message)

EATING DISORDERS

Overeaters Anonymous
National Office
P.O. Box 44020
Rio Rancho, NM 87174-4020
(505) 891-2664

GAMBLING

Gamblers Anonymous
New York Intergroup
P.O. Box 7
New York, NY 10116-0007
(212) 903-4400

HEALTH ISSUES

Alzheimer's Association
919 N. Michigan Ave., Ste. 1100
Chicago, IL 60611-1676
(800) 621-0379

**American Chronic Pain
Association**
P.O. Box 850
Rocklin, CA 95677
(916) 632-0922
www.theacpa.org

American Holistic Health Association
P.O. Box 17400
Anaheim, CA 92817
(714) 779-6152
e-mail: ahha.org
www.ahha@healthy.net

Chopra Center for Well Being
Deepak Chopra, M.D.
www.chopra.com

The Fetzer Institute
9292 West KL Ave.
Kalamazoo, MI 49009
(616) 375-2000

Hippocrates Health Institute
1443 Palmdale Court
West Palm Beach, FL 33411

Hospicelink
190 Westbrook Rd.
Essex, CN 06426
(800) 331-1620

Institute for Noetic Sciences
P.O. Box 909
Sausalito, CA 94966
(415) 331-5650

The Mind-Body Medical Institute
110 Francis St., Ste. 1A
Boston, MA 02215
(617) 632-9525

National Health Information Center
P.O. Box 1133
Washington, DC 20013-1133
(800) 336-4797

Optimum Health Care Institute
6970 Central Ave.
Lemon Grove, CA 91945
(619) 464-3346

Preventive Medicine Research Institute
Dean Ornish, M.D.
900 Bridgeway, Ste. 2
Sausalito, CA 94965
(415) 332-2525

HOUSING RESOURCES

Acorn
(nonprofit network of low- and moderate-income housing)
739 8th St., S.E.
Washington, DC 20003
(202) 547-9292

IMPOTENCE

Impotence Institute of America
P.O. Box 410
Bowie, MD 20718-0410
(800) 669-1603
www.impotenceworld.org

MENTAL HEALTH

American Psychiatric Association of America
www.psych.org

Anxiety Disorders Association of America
www.adaa.org

The Help Center of the American Psychological Association
www.helping.apa.org

The International Society for Mental Health Online
www.ismho.org

Knowledge Exchange Network
www.mentalhealth.org

National Center for Post-Traumatic Stress Disorder (PTSD)
www.dartmouth.edu/dms/ptsd

National Alliance for the Mentally Ill
www.nami.org

National Depressive and Manic-Depressive Association
www.ndmda.org

National Institute of Mental Health
www.nimh.nih.gov

PET BEREAVEMENT

Bide-A-Wee Foundation
410 E. 38th St.
New York, NY 10016
(212) 532-6395

Holistic Animal Consulting Centre
29 Lyman Ave.
Staten Island, NY 10305
(718) 720-5548

RAPE/SEXUAL ISSUES

Rape, Abuse, and Incest National Network
(800) 656-4673

Safe Place
P.O. Box 19454
Austin, TX 78760
(512) 440-7273

National Council on Sexual Addictions and Compulsivity
1090 S. Northchase Parkway, Ste. 200
South Marietta, GA 30067
(770) 989-9754

Sexually Transmitted Disease Referral
(800) 227-8922

SMOKING

Nicotine Anonymous
P.O. Box 126338
Harrisburg, PA 17112
(415) 750-0328
www.nicotine-anonymous.org

STRESS REDUCTION

The Biofeedback & Psychophysiology Clinic
The Menninger Clinic
P.O. Box 829
Topeka, KS 66601-0829
(913) 350-5000

New York Open Center
(In-depth workshops to invigorate the spirit)
83 Spring St.
New York, NY 10012
(212) 219-2527

Omega Institute
(a healing, spiritual retreat community)
150 Lake Dr.
Rhinebeck, NY 12572-3212
(845) 266-4444 (info)
(800) 944-1001 (to enroll)

The Stress Reduction Clinic
Center for Mindfulness
University of Massachusetts
Medical Center
55 Lake Ave. North
Worcester, MA 01655
(508) 856-1616
(508) 856-2656

TEEN HELP

ADOL: Adolescent Directory Online
Includes information on eating disorders, depression, and teen pregnancy.
www.education.indiana.edu/cas/adol/adol.html

Al-Anon/Alateen
1600 Corporate Landing Parkway
Virginia Beach, VA 23454-5617
(888) 425-2666
(888) 4AL-ANON
www.al-anon.org

Focus Adolescent Services:
Eating Disorders
www.focusas.com/
EatingDisorders.html

Future Point
A nonprofit organization that
offers message boards and chat
rooms to empower teens in the
academic world and beyond.
www.futurepoint.org

Kids in Trouble Help Page
Child abuse, depression, suicide,
and runaway resources, with
links and hotline numbers.
www.geocities.com/
EnchantedForest/2910

Planned Parenthood
810 Seventh Ave.
New York, NY 10019
(212) 541-7800
www.plannedparenthood.org

SafeTeens.com
Provides lessons on online
safety and privacy; also has
resources for homework and
fun on the web.
www.safeteens.com

TeenCentral.net
This site is written by and about
teens. Includes celebrity stories,
real-teen tales, an anonymous
help line, and crisis counseling.
www.teencentral.net

TeenOutReach.com
Includes all kinds of information geared at teens, from sports
to entertainment to help with
drugs and eating disorders.
www.teenoutreach.com

Hotlines for Teenagers

Boys Town National Hotline
(800) 448-3000

**Childhelp National Child Abuse
Hotline/**
Voices for Children
(800) 422-4453
(800) 4ACHILD

Just for Kids Hotline
(888) 594-5437
(888) 594-KIDS

National Child Abuse Hotline
(800) 792-5200

National Runaway Hotline
(800) 621-4000

National Youth Crisis Hotline
(800) 442-4673
(800) 442-HOPE

Suicide Prevention Hotline
(800) 827-7571

Bibliography

Abcarian, R., Post-Quake Quirk Is Something to Chew On, *Los Angeles Times*, January 30, 1994, E-6–E-7.

Anderson, G. H. & Leiter, L. A. (1988), Effects of Aspartame and Phenylalanine on Meal-Time Food Intake of Humans, *Appetite,* Vol. 11S, pp. 48–53.

Armsworth, M. W. (1990), A Qualitative Analysis of Adult Incest Survivors' Responses to Sexual Involvement with Therapists, *Child Abuse & Neglect,* Vol. 14, pp. 541–554.

Beattie, H. J. (1988), Eating Disorders and the Mother-Daughter Relationship, *International Journal of Eating Disorders*, Vol. 7, No. 4, pp. 453–460.

Behr, E., *The Complete Book of Les Miserables.* New York: Arcade Publishing, 1989.

Benward, J. & Densen-Gerber, J. (1975), Incest As a Causative Factor in Antisocial Behavior: An Explanatory Study. *Contemporary Drug Problems*, Vol. 4, pp. 323–346.

Bowie, S. I., et al. (1990), Blitz Rape and Confidence Rape: Implications for Clinical Intervention. *American Journal of Psychotherapy*, Vol. XLIV, No. 2, 180–188.

Bownes, I. T., et al. (1990), Assault Characteristics and Post-traumatic Stress Disorder in Rape Victims, *Acta Psychiatric Scandanavia*, Vol. 83, pp. 27–30.

Bricklin, M. (1993), Destress Your Tummy Away. *Prevention*, Vol. 45, No. 11.

Burgess, A. (1985), *The Sexual Victimization of Adolescents.* Washington, D.C.: National Center for the Prevention and Control of Rape.

Calam, R. M. & Slade, P. D. (1989), Sexual Experience and Eating Problems in Female Undergraduates, *International Journal of Eating Disorders*, Vol. 8, No. 4, pp. 391–397.

Cattanach, M. & Rodin, J. (1988), Psychosocial Components of the Stress Process in Bulimia, *International Journal of Eating Disorders*, Vol. 7, No. 1, pp. 75–88.

Cavaiola, A. A. & Schiff, M. (1989), Self-Esteem In Abused Chemically-Dependent Adolescents, *Child Abuse & Neglect*, Vol. 13, pp. 327–334.

Chaouloff, F., et al. (1989), Physical Exercise: Evidence for Differential Consequences of Tryptophan on 5-HT Synthesis and Metabolism in Central Serotonergic Cell Bodies and Terminals, *Journal of Neural Transmission*, Vol. 78, pp. 121–130.

Chu, J. A. & Dill, D. L. (1990), Dissociative Symptoms in Relation to Childhood Physical and Sexual Abuse, *American Journal of Psychiatry*, Vol. 147, No. 7, pp. 887–891.

Cohen, F. S. & Densen-Gerber, J. (1982), A Study of the Relationship Between Child Abuse and Drug Addiction in 178 Patients: Preliminary Results. *Child Abuse & Neglect*, No. 6, pp. 383–387.

Cornell, W. & Olio, K. (1991), Integrating Affect in Treatment with Adult Survivors of Physical and Sexual Abuse, *American Journal of Orthopsychiatry*, Vol. 61, No. 1, pp. 59–69.

Daie, N., et al. (1989), Long-Term Effects of Sibling Incest. *Journal of Clinical Psychiatry*, Vol. 50, No. 11, pp. 428–431.

Devine, R. (1980), *Incest: A Review of the Literature. In Sexual Abuse of Children: Selected Readings.* Washington, D. C.: U.S. Department of Health and Human Services, DHHS Publication No. (OHDS) 78-30161.

Dyer, J. B. & Crouch, J. G. (1988), Effects of Running and Other Activities On Moods, *Perceptual and Motor Skills*, Vol. 67, No. 43–50.

Dyer, W.W., *Everyday Wisdom*. Carlsbad, California: Hay House, 1993.

Felitti, V. J., Long-Term Medical Consequences of Incest, Rape and Molestation, *Southern Medical Journal*, Vol. 84, No. 3, pp. 328–331.

Fernstrom, J. D. (1988), Carbohydrate Ingestion and Brain Serotonin Synthesis: Relevance to a Putative Control Loop for Regulating Carbohydrate Ingestion, and Effects of Aspartame Consumption, *Appetite*, Vol. 11S, pp. 35–41.

Frankl, V. E., *Man's Search for Meaning*. Boston: Beacon Press, 1962.

Friedman, S. R. (1990), What Is Child Sexual Abuse? *Journal of Clinical Psychology*, Vol. 46, No. 3, pp. 372–397.

Gardner, R. M., et al. (1991), Body Image of Sexually and Physically Abused Children. *Journal of Psychiatry*, Vol. 24, No. 4, pp. 313–321.

Goldfarb, L. A. (1987), Sexual Abuse Antecedent to Anorexia Nervosa, Bulimia, and Compulsive Overeating: Three Case Reports, *International Journal of Eating Disorders,* Vol. 6, No. 5, pp. 675–680.

Goldsmith, S. J., et al. (1992), Psychiatric Illness in Patients Presenting for Obesity Treatment, *International Journal of Eating Disorders*, Vol. 12, No. 1, pp. 63–71.

Gordon, B. N., et al., (1990), Children's Knowledge of Sexuality: A Comparison of Sexually Abused and Nonabused Children, *American Journal of Orthopsychiatry*, Vol. 60, No. 2, pp. 250–257.

Greenwald, E., et al. (1990), Childhood Sexual Abuse: Long-Term Effects on Psychological and Sexual Functioning In A Non-Clinical and Non-Student Sample of Adult Women, *Child Abuse & Neglect*, Vol. 14, pp. 503–513.

Hay, Louise L., *Heal Your Body: The Mental Causes for Physical Illness and the Metaphysical Way to Overcome Them* (Revised Edition). Carlsbad, California: Hay House, 1988.

———, *You Can Heal Your Life*. Carlsbad, California: Hay House, 1984.

Henriksen, S., et al. (1974), The Role of Serotonin in the Regulation of a Phasic Event of Rapid Eye Movement Sleep: The Ponto-geniculo-occipital Wave, *Advances in Biochemical Psychopharmacology,* Vol. 11, pp. 169—179.

Kopp, S., *Raise Your Right Hand Against Fear!* Minneapolis: CompCare Publishers, 1989.

Ladwig, G. B. & Andersen, M. D. (1989), Substance Abuse in Women: Relationship Between Chemical Dependency of Women and Past Reports of Physical and/or Sexual Abuse, *The International Journal of the Addictions*, Vol. 24, Vol. 8, pp. 739–754.

Mackey, T. F., et al. (1991), Comparative Effects of Sexual Assault on Sexual Functioning of Child Sexual Abuse Survivors and Others, *Issues in Mental Health Nursing*, Vol. 12, pp. 89–112.

Marano, H. E. (1993), Chemistry & Craving. *Psychology Today*, Vol. 26, No. 1.

Martin, S., et al. (1988), Self-Esteem of Adolescent Girls as Related To Weight, *Perceptual and Motor Skills*, Vol. 67, pp. 879–884.

May, R., *The Meaning of Anxiety*. New York: W.W. Norton, 1977 (Revised Edition).

Morgan, E. & Froning, M. (1989), Child Sexual Abuse Sequelae and Body-Image Surgery, *Plastic and Reconstructive Surgery*, Vol. 86, No. 3, pp. 475–478.

Mynors-Wallis, L. (1992), et al., Life Events and Anorexia Nervosa: Differences Between Early and Late Onset Cases, *International Journal of Eating Disorders*, Vol. 11, No. 4, pp. 369–375.

Neergaard, L., When It Comes to Fitness, Americans Prefer Lazy Way, *The Orange County Register,* November 7, 1993.

Ogata, S. N., et al. (1990), Childhood Sexual and Physical Abuse in Adult Patients with Borderline Personality Disorder, *American Journal of Psychiatry*, Vol. 147, No. 8, pp. 1008–1012.

Oppenheimer, R., et al. (1985), Adverse Sexual Experience in Childhood and Clinical Eating Disorders: A Preliminary Description, *Journal of Psychiatry*, Vol. 19, No. 2/3, pp. 357–361.

Paddison, P. L., et al. (1990), Sexual Abuse and Premenstrual Syndrome: Comparison Between a Lower and Higher Socioeconomic Group, *Psychosomatics*, Vol. 31, No. 3, pp. 265–271.

Peale, N. V., *The Positive Principle Today*. New York: Prentice-Hall, 1976.

Pennington, J. & Church, H. N., *Food Values of Portions Commonly Used*, 14th Edition. New York: Harper & Row Publishers, 1985.

Peterson, S., Weighed Down By Prejudice?, *Orange County Register*, September 30, 1993, pp. 1– 6.

Rand, C. & Kuldau, J. (1989), The Epidemiology of Obesity and Self-Defined Weight Problem in the General Population: Gender, Age, and Social Class, *International Journal of Eating Disorders*, Vol. 9, No. 3, pp. 329–343.

Rohsenow, D. J., et al. (1988), Molested As Children: A Hidden Contribution to Substance Abuse? *Journal of Substance Abuse Treatment*, Vol. 5, pp. 18–19.

Root, M. P. (1989), Treatment Failures: The Role of Sexual Victimization in Women's Addictive Behavior, *American Journal of Orthopsychiatry*, Vol. 59, No. 4, pp. 542–549.

Rosen, J. C., et al. (1990), Life Stress, Psychological Symptoms and Weight Reducing Behavior in Adolescent Girls: A Prospective Analysis, *International Journal of Eating Disorders*, Vol. 9, No. 1, pp. 17–26.

Schuman, M., et al. (1990), Sweets, Chocolate and Atypical Depressive Traits, *The Journal of Nervous and Mental Disease*, Vol. 175, pp. 491–499.

Shapiro, S. & Dominiak, G. (1990), Common Psychological Defenses Seen in the Treatment of Sexually-Abused Adolescents, *American Journal of Psychotherapy*, Vol. XLIV, No. 1, pp. 68–74.

Singer, M. I., et al. (1989) The Relationship Between Sexual Abuse and Substance Abuse Among Psychiatrically Hospitalized Adolescents, *Child Abuse & Neglect*, Vol. 13, pp. 319–325.

Smolak, L., et al. (1990), Are Child Sexual Experiences Related to Eating-Disordered Attitudes and Behaviors in a College Sample?, *International Journal of Eating Disorders*, Vol. 9, No. 2, pp. 167–178.

Strober, M. (1984), Stressful Life Events Associated with Bulimia in Anorexia Nervosa, *International Journal of Eating Disorders*, Vol. 3, No. 2, pp. 3–15.

Surrey, J., et al. (1990), Reported History of Physical and Sexual Abuse and Severity of Symptomatology in Women Psychiatric Outpatients, *American Journal of Orthopsychiatry*, Vol. 60, No. 3, pp. 412–417.

Terr, L. C. (1991), Childhood Traumas: An Outline and Overview, *American Journal of Psychiatry*, Vol. 148, No. 1, pp. 10–19.

Tice, L., et al. (1989), Sexual Abuse in Patients with Eating Disorders, *Psychiatric Medicine,* Vol. 7, No. 4, pp. 257–267.

Virtue, D. L., *The Chocoholic's Dream Diet.* First Edition: Bantam, 1990, Second Edition: Century-Guild Press, 1994.

————, *The Yo-Yo Syndrome Diet.* New York: Harper-Collins, 1990.

————, *My Kids Don't Live with Me Anymore: Coping with the Custody Crisis.* Minneapolis, Minn.: CompCare, 1988.

Wallace, R., Survey: Good Grades Don't Give Immunity from Sexual Assaults, *The Orange County Register,* December 1, 1993, p. 6(A).

Weingourt, R. (1990), Wife Rape in a Sample of Psychiatric Patients, Image: *Journal of Nursing Scholarship*, Vol. 22, No. 3, pp. 144–147.

Wendel, G. & Lester, D. (1988), Body-Cathesis and Self-Esteem, *Perceptual and Motor Skills,* Vol. 67, pp. 538–545.

Wurtman, J. (1982), Studies on the Appetite for Carbohydrates in Rats and Humans, *Journal of Psychiatry*, Vol. 17, No. 2, pp. 213–221.

Wurtman, R. J. & Wurtman, J. (1988), Do Carbohydrates Affect Food Intake Via Neurotransmitter Activity?, *Appetite*, Vol. 11S, pp. 42–47.

Young, E. B., The Role of Incest Issues in Relapse, *Journal of Psychoactive Drugs*, Vol. 22, No. 2, pp. 249–257.

About the Author

Doreen Virtue, Ph.D., is a spiritual doctor of psychology, and the former director of two all-women psychiatric hospitals specializing in abuse issues. She holds a B.A., M.A., and Ph.D. in counseling psychology, and her doctoral dissertation was on the link between childhood abuse histories and the subsequent development of an eating disorder.

Dr. Virtue's work has been featured in *Redbook, Woman's Day, Vegetarian Times, Shape, Fitness,* and other magazines. She has appeared on *Oprah,* CNN, *Good Morning America, The View with Barbara Walters,* and many other shows.

In 1995, following Divine intervention, Dr. Virtue stopped her practice of traditional psychotherapy and began working as an angel therapist. She writes about her transition, as well as her discoveries in spiritual healing methods, in her books *The Lightworker's Way* and *Healing with the Angels.* Dr. Virtue gives workshops on spiritual topics throughout the world. For information on her workshops; or other books, tapes, and oracle cards, please visit her Website at: **www.AngelTherapy.com**

Dr. Virtue no longer practices psychotherapy. She is, therefore, unable to give referrals to eating-disorder therapists and answer questions about this topic. However, you can direct questions to Becky Prelitz, R.D., M.F.T., the co-author with Dr. Virtue of the book *Eating in the Light* (Hay House, 2001). You can contact Becky by e-mail at: **byondfood@aol.com**. Becky offers spiritually and nutritionally based group and individual counseling to those with food and weight concerns. She is also available for consultations by telephone and e-mail.

Other Hay House Titles
of Related Interest

Books

BodyChange™: *The 21-Day Fitness Program for Changing Your Body and Changing Your Life,* by Montel Williams and Wini Linguvic

Dr. Citron's Evolutionary Diet, by Ronald S. Citron, M.D., and Kathye J. Citron

Eating in the Light: *Making the Switch to Vegetarianism on Your Spiritual Path,* by Doreen Virtue, Ph.D., and Becky Prelitz, R.D., M.F.T.

Gut Feelings: From Fear and Despair to Health and Hope, by Carnie Wilson

Heal Your Body A–Z, by Louise L. Hay

Vegetarian Meals for People-on-the-Go: *101 Quick & Easy Recipes,* by Vimala Rodgers

The Yo-Yo Diet Syndrome, by Doreen Virtue, Ph.D.

Audio Programs

Body Talk: *No-Nonsense, Common-Sense Solutions to Create Health and Healing,* by Mona Lisa Schulz, M.D., Ph.D., and Christiane Northrup, M.D.

Eating Wisdom, by Andrew Weil, M.D., with Michael Toms

Healing Your Appetite, Healing Your Life, by Doreen Virtue, Ph.D.

Live Long and Feel Good, by Andrew Weil, M.D.

Your Diet, Your Health, by Christiane Northrup, M.D.

All of the above are available at your local bookstore,
or may be ordered through Hay House, Inc.:
(800) 654-5126 or **(760) 431-7695**
(800) 650-5115 (fax) or **(760) 431-6948 (fax)**

We hope you enjoyed this Hay House book.
If you would like to receive a free catalog featuring additional
Hay House books and products, or if you would like informa-
tion about the Hay Foundation, please contact:

Hay House, Inc.
P.O. Box 5100
Carlsbad, CA 92018-5100

(760) 431-7695 or **(800) 654-5126**
(760) 431-6948 (fax) or **(800) 650-5115 (fax)**

Hay House Australia Pty Ltd
P.O. Box 515
Brighton-Le-Sands NSW 2216
phone: 1800 023 516
e-mail: info@hayhouse.com.au

Please visit the Hay House Website at: **www.hayhouse.com**